FORMULA 1

THE COMPLETE HISTORY OF F1 THROUGH THE YEARS

igloobooks

CONTAINS
COLLECTABLE
MEMORABILIA

igloobooks

Published in 2016
by Igloo Books Ltd
Cottage Farm
Sywell
NN6 0BJ
www.igloobooks.com

GUA006 0616
2 4 6 8 10 9 7 5 3
ISBN 978-1-78440-262-4

Front cover image © Clive Mason / Getty Images
Back cover image © Thinkstock / Getty Images

Printed and manufactured in China

FORMULA 1

THE COMPLETE HISTORY OF F1 THROUGH THE YEARS

Contents

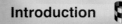

Introduction

No sooner had the first motor cars been developed at the end of the 19th century than drivers started competing to see who could go further and faster. In 1894 the Paris to Rouen trial saw 21 cars competing for a 5,000 Franc first prize, which was awarded jointly to Panhard et Levassor and Peugeot for displaying the best combination of safety, economy, and ease of driving. It was a popular event and the following year, 1895, what is now held to be the world's first motor race was devised.

Formula One is still the world's greatest motorsport series. It's exciting, exhilarating, prestigious, and the only championship that is genuinely global in its reach.

LEFT: Sebastian Vettel (Toro Rosso STR03 Ferrari) in action during the 2008 Japanese Grand Prix at the Fuji Speedway.

The Circuits

Formula One is the premier, international racing series, so hosting the races in different countries demands suitable circuits for the drivers to play out their championships. Over the course of Formula One's history, the circuits have been agreed by royals, heads of state, governments, television and media producers, and even key sports people, but always through the Fédération Internationale du Sport Automobile (FISA) and in conjunction with the FIA.

LEFT: An aerial view of the Silverstone circuit before the 2006 British Grand Prix.

9

Abu Dhabi Grand Prix

YAS MARINA CIRCUIT

The Abu Dhabi Grand Prix made its debut during the 2009 Formula One season and has grown to be one of the most popular circuits, with a sell-out crowd of around 50,000 expected for the 2013 race. The capital of the United Arab Emirates, Abu Dhabi's wealth derives from the fact that it is one of the world's largest producers of oil. This makes it perfectly matched to partner the financially unconstrained Formula One.

Yas Marina Circuit cost $1,200 million to build and was designed by Hermann Tilke, who overhauled numerous European circuits, including Hockenheimring. As well as a stunning race track, the development is based around a harbor and includes a theme park, water park, residential areas, hotels, restaurants and beaches.

Yas Marina Circuit also contains a permanent lighting system and holds the title of the largest permanent lighting sports venue in the world. This lighting was used in the inaugural race of 2009, making it also the first day–night race. The surface of the track itself contains aggregate from Bayston Hill, a quarry in Shropshire, England.

The track boasts the longest straight in the current Formula One calendar and has a unique pit lane exit, where the cars pass through a tunnel under the track and emerge at Turn 3. In 2009, Giancarlo Fisichella expressed his displeasure at this uniqueness by claiming it was difficult and therefore potentially dangerous.

There are twenty-one corners which twist around the man-made island, passing iconic architecture hotels such as the Yas Viceroy Hotel as well as winding through sand dunes, five high speed stretches, and five slow turns with three ideal spots for overtaking.

Right: Yas Marina Formula One Circuit Racing Track in Abu Dhabi, United Arab Emirates.

>>>>

YAS MARINA CIRCUIT

TYPE:	permanent circuit
LOCATION:	Yas Island, 15m (25km) northeast of Abu Dhabi, UAE
CIRCUIT LENGTH:	3.45 miles (5.55 km)
LAP RECORD:	1:40.279 (S Vettel/Red Bull 2009)

Racing to Turn 1, drivers can achieve a speed of around 95 mph (154 kph) in gear 4 with a resulting G-force of around 3–4. The left-hand turn is quite tricky and a lot faster than it would at first appear. Exiting Turn 1 is an uphill climb taken very fast with a challenging left and right sequence of corners before going downhill and past grandstand stadiums and into a slow left hand corner. This corner emerges onto a very long back straight, which at the end requires very hard braking into a left-hand and right-hand corner; drivers have to be neat through these corners to be in a good position for another long straight. After the straight is an overtaking opportunity in the 2nd gear left-hand corner, preceding a slow chicane and then into a sequence of very slow corners, first a right followed by a left going under the Yas Viceroy Hotel and a left coming out. This is followed by a quick right-hand corner before the pit lane entrance on the right, and then a final right-hand corner with a straight to the grandstand finish.

In its early years, the racing was criticized for the lack of overtaking opportunities in the tight turns of the second half of the lap and failed to live up to its spectacular surroundings. However, 2012's grand prix was an exciting, fraught event filled with collisions. Lap 20 was where the race leader Lewis Hamilton exited as a result of a technical issue with his McLaren. Kimi Räikkönen inherited the lead and, despite heroic attempts by Alonso and Vettel, Räikkönen went on to win his first race since his Formula One comeback. His radio conversation at the time with his engineer will forever be remembered as he exclaimed, "Leave me alone, I know what I'm doing."

Below: The grid shell of the Yas Viceroy Hotel has become an iconic symbol of Abu Dhabi's Grand Prix.

0002234.56
450.4
99834568.23
44567.343
366585

Fernando Alonso drives during the third practice session at the Yas Marina circuit on November 3, 2012 in Abu Dhabi ahead of the Abu Dhabi Formula One Grand Prix.

Argentine Grand Prix

AUTÓDROME OSCAR JUAN Y GÁLVEZ

The Autódromo Oscar Juan y Gálvez in Buenos Aires has not been used for the Argentine Grand Prix since 1998, despite its fine facilities. Instead, it is now used both for national motor racing meetings and for hosting major outdoor events.

The track was first developed in 1952 by Argentine President Juan Péron, who wanted to attract the world's attention to the achievements of the country's best known and most successful racing driver, Juan Manuel Fangio. The circuit was duly constructed on what had been marshland just outside Buenos Aires.

When it was first opened, the circuit consisted of a newly built inner circuit combined with some existing local roads, creating a 3.6 mile (5.75 km) track with 15 turns. After being extended to include a lakeside section with two fast straights (Recto del Longo and Recto del Lago) it became the first truly international racing circuit in South America.

In the very last Formula One race held at the circuit, in 1998, David Coulthard took pole position though the race itself was won by Michael Schumacher. After that, financial problems made it impossible for further races to be held in Buenos Aires.

Below: Giuseppe Farina (Ferrari 625/555) leads Karl Kling (Mercedes-Benz W196) during the 1955 Argentine Grand Prix.

⌄ ⌄ ⌄ ⌄

60

⦿ AUTÓDROMO OSCAR ALFREDO GÁLVEZ

TYPE:	purpose-built
LOCATION:	Buenos Aires
CIRCUIT LENGTH:	3.61 miles (5.81 km)
LAP RECORD:	1:27.981 (G Berger/Benetton-Renault 1997)

Australian Grand Prix

ALBERT PARK

Following safety concerns after a high-speed accident in free practice in Adelaide in 1995, the Australian Grand Prix moved to Albert Park in Melbourne. At the time, officials in Australia were negotiating to bring the Pacific Grand Prix to the country, which, with their own Australian Grand Prix, would have given them two races.

Situated only around a mile from the skyscrapers of the Central Business District, the Melbourne Grand Prix's 3.29 mile (5.29 km) circuit backdrop consists of public roads. Despite its 16 corners, it is one of the fastest street circuits in the world, with top speeds of over 185 mph (300 kph), and average lap times of around 140 mph (225 kph). Because the track consists of conventional road tarmac, traction in the early stages of the Grand Prix weekend is always an issue until a "racing line" is laid down over the course of the race weekend. It's also a tough track for both drivers and machinery since as many as 3,500 gear-changes are made during the race and full-throttle is used for three-quarters of an average lap. Further difficulties are caused by the fact that the track is bumpy and has very limited run-off areas, so a sound chassis is essential for success and to avoid making high-speed contact with the walls.

Right: Lewis Hamilton, (McLaren MP4-23 Mercedes) leads during the 2008 Australian Grand Prix at Albert Park.

>>>>

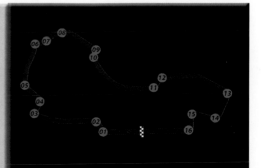

ALBERT PARK

TYPE:	city park
LOCATION:	Melbourne, Australia
CIRCUIT LENGTH:	3.29 miles (5.29 km)
LAP RECORD:	1:24.125
	(M Schumacher/Ferrari 2004)

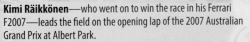

Kimi Räikkönen—who went on to win the race in his Ferrari F2007—leads the field on the opening lap of the 2007 Australian Grand Prix at Albert Park.

Austrian Grand Prix

A1 Ring

With the Alps creating a backbone for much of Austria, it comes as no surprise to discover that the A1-Ring, near Spielberg, is far from flat. In fact, it was developed using part of the winding and very fast Österreichring, which was renowned for its hilly terrain.

The A1-Ring is a very fast circuit with only ten corners during its 2.68 miles (4.31 km) lap. It also boasts four straights, and even though two of them have slight kinks, the circuit sees drivers revving right up to the red line and reaching speeds of up to 190 mph (304 kph) before going hard on the brakes for a succession of epic corners, including the Remus, Gösser, Niki Lauda, Jochen Rindt, and Castrol Kurves.

Formula One first came to the A1-Ring in 1997 after Hermann Tilke thoroughly revised the circuit, though concerns about safety resulted in it later losing its

place on the F1 calendar in 2003. The circuit itself is now owned by Dietrick Mateschitz, owner of the Red Bull energy drink and the Formula One teams named after it. However, attempts to bring Formula One back to the A1-Ring have failed despite repeated efforts by Mateschitz to attract top level racing back.

Below: Michael Schumacher (Ferrari F2003 GA) punches the air to celebrate his race win during the 2003 Austrian Grand Prix at A1-Ring.

◯ A1 RING

TYPE:	purpose-built
LOCATION:	Spielberg, Austria
CIRCUIT LENGTH:	2.68 miles (4.31 km)
LAP RECORD:	1:08.337
	(M Schumacher/Ferrari 2003)

*B*ahrain *Grand Prix*

BAHRAIN INTERNATIONAL CIRCUIT

Right: Takuma Sato (BAR   >>>>
Honda 006) leads Jenson
Button (BAR Honda 006)
into turn one of the 2004
Bahrain Grand Prix.

The Bahrain International Circuit
was the worthy recipient of the
inaugural FIA Institute Center
of Excellence Trophy in 2007.
First opened in 2004 following
an investment of some $150
million, it's a state-of-the-art
motorsport circuit built in the
desert around 20 miles (32
km) south of Bahrain's capital
Manama.

The 3.36 miles (5.41 km) lap of the Grand Prix track
consists of 15 corners and four straights, the longest
of which is 1,192 yards (1,090 m) from start to finish.
There's plenty of variation, as the track rises and
falls nearly 20 yards (18 m) and varies in width from
15 to 24 yards (14 to 22 m). Created from scratch
out in the desert, construction involved excavating
34 million square feet (968,459 cubic meters) of
rock; laying 132,000 tonnes (120,000 metric tons)
of asphalt and 18.5 million gallons (70,000 cubic
meters) of concrete; erecting 13,000 yards (12,000
m) of guard rails and 5,500 yards (5,000 m) of

FIA safety fencing; placing 82,000 tires, and even
laying 6,000 square yards (5,000 square meters) of
grass carpet.

When it hosted the 2004 race, Bahrain was the very
first Grand Prix to be held in the Middle East. The
2012 Grand Prix was one of the most controversial
races in Formula One history when it went ahead
despite political unrest, protests and human rights
organizations calling for the race to be boycotted.

BAHRAIN INTERNATIONAL CIRCUIT

TYPE:	purpose-built
LOCATION:	Manama, Bahrain
CIRCUIT LENGTH:	3.36 miles (5.41 km)
LAP RECORD:	1:32.408
	(Nico Rosberg/
	Williams-Cosworth 2006)

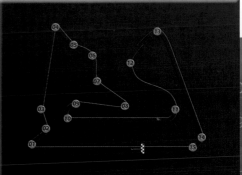

Caterham Renault practicing changing tyres and refueling in the Pits on April 18, 2013, Bahrain Grand Prix 2013.

F1

Belgian Grand Prix

SPA

Spa-Francorchamps is located in Belgium's beautiful Ardennes Forest region, close to the German border.

It now boasts the longest lap of any Grand Prix circuit at 4.34 miles (6.98 km), which incorporates part of a local main road that is understandably closed to traffic during the race weekend. From the start/finish line, drivers accelerate first to La Source hairpin, often the scene of first-lap incidents, before speeding through the steep downhill section leading to the Raidillon chicane.

Next comes a long, steep uphill climb along the Kemmel Straight and through Les Combs, a complex

succession of right-left-right bends that require a perfectly balanced suspension and nerves of steel from the driver. Next comes a further fast downhill section to the Rivage hairpin, followed by a left into the short Malmedy straight, another left through Pouhon and then a further series of bends.

The driver then reaches the fast Curve Paul Frere and then onto the public road to Blanchmont, the fastest point of the circuit. It's then hard on the brakes for the chicane which replaced the famous "Bus-stop," and then back onto the start/finish straight.

Along with the Suzuka circuit in Japan, Spa-Francorchamps is generally considered to be one of the world's most challenging circuits.

Above: Michael Schumacher (Ferrari F310) makes his way through Eau Rouge at Spa-Francorchamps during the 1996 Belgian Grand Prix.

⬤ SPA-FRANCORCHAMPS

TYPE:	purpose-built parkland
LOCATION:	Spa, Belgium
CIRCUIT LENGTH:	4.34 miles (6.98 km)
LAP RECORD:	1:45.108 (K Raikkonen/ McLaren-Mercedes 2004)

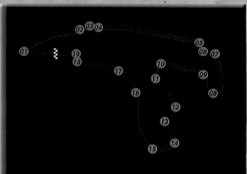

Brazilian Grand Prix

AUTÓDROMO JOSÉ CARLOS PACE

The current home of the Brazilian round of the World Formula One Championship—always an exciting event because it's normally the last event of the year where the Drivers or Constructors Championships are often decided— is the Autódromo José Carlos Pace, Interlagos. It is located in the suburbs 11 miles (17.7 km) south of the city of São Paolo.

Before 1980, the Interlagos Grand Prix circuit got its name from it's located between two large lakes. It fell out of favor, however, because of its close proximity to extensive favelas—slums— which were not felt to reflect Formula One's glamorous values, so the race was removed to Rio de Janeiro until 1990, after which the Grand Prix circus returned to a remodeled Interlagos.

The start/finish straight leads into a tricky downhill series of bends that have ended many drivers' races on lap one. Unusually in Formula One, the Interlagos circuit runs counter-clockwise which can cause difficulties for drivers more used to clockwise circuits. Car set-up is crucial for success at this challenging circuit as engineers have to try to balance power with downforce and aerodynamic efficiency. To make matters even more difficult, the circuit is tough on cars, too, because of its abrasive surface; because São Paolo is set at nearly 2,500 feet (760 m) the thinner air reduces power output by 8 percent. However, this is one of the rare Formula One circuits where overtaking opportunities are plentiful.

Above: Felipe Massa (Ferrari F2008) in first position at the start of the 2008 Brazilian Grand Prix at Interlagos.

Right: Carlos Pace (Brabham BT44B Ford) during the 1975 Brazilian Grand Prix at Interlagos: this was to be his first and only Grand Prix win.>>>>

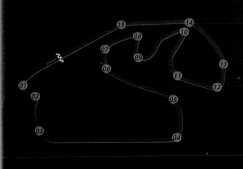

AUTÓDROMO JOSÉ CARLOS PACE, INTERLAGOS

TYPE:	purpose-built
LOCATION:	Interlagos, São Paolo, Brazil
CIRCUIT LENGTH:	2.667 miles (4.29 km)
LAP RECORD:	1:11.473 (JP Montoya/Williams-BMW 2004)

Lewis Hamilton (R) of Great Britain, McLaren and team mate Jenson Button (L) of Great Britain, McLaren drive side-by-side during the Brazilian Formula One Grand Prix at the Autódromo José Carlos Pace.

British Grand Prix

SILVERSTONE

There is a large sign outside the gates of Silverstone that proudly declares that this is "The Home of British Motorsport." When the Royal Automobile Club started looking for a venue where motor racing activities could be restarted, the disused airfields of Silverstone on the Northamptonshire/Buckinghamshire border looked ideal.

The original track was 3.67 miles (5.9 km) long. A chicane was added in 1975 to slow drivers before the notorious Woodcote Corner and changes were made at Bridge in 1987. In 1990/91, a major redesign resulted in the creation of the Luffield Complex and introduced some elevation to other parts of the track.

Despite the changes, Silverstone remains one of the fastest of all Grand Prix circuits, and during the Grand Prix weekend its main runway becomes Britain's busiest airport and heliport. From the start opposite the pits there's a fast right-hander at Copse which is followed by Maggotts, Becketts, and Chapel curves. Then it's into the extremely fast Hangar Straight, at the end of which is Stowe Corner, followed by the dip into Vale and a very challenging 90-degree left and the gradually unwinding right of Club Corner. After Abbey Curve, there's the short Farm Straight, then under Bridge for first Priory, followed by Luffield and finally Woodcote, and back on to the start/finish straight.

Right: Jean Alesi (Benetton B196 Renault) leads Mika Häkkinen (McLaren MP4/11 Mercedes) and Michael Schumacher (Ferrari F310) during the 1996 British Grand Prix at Silverstone. >>>>>>>>>

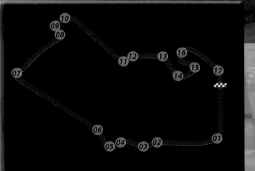

SILVERSTONE CIRCUIT

TYPE:	purpose-built airfield
LOCATION:	Silverstone, England
CIRCUIT LENGTH:	3.18 miles (5.12 km)
LAP RECORD:	1:18.739 (M Schumacher/Ferrari 2004)

0002234.567
450.45
99834568.234
44567.3431
3665854
35657686.575

Virgin sponsored Brawn Formula One car at Silverstone circuit
July 10, 2011, British Grand Prix.

British Grand Prix

BRANDS HATCH

Brands Hatch, in Kent, in the southeast of England is one of the truly great British motor racing venues. Its location, 20 miles (32 km) southeast of London, was a perfect spectator draw.

At the end of the start/finish straight is the blind Paddock Hill Bend right-hander which falls away sharply, before rising up Hailwood Hill to Druids Bend. Then it's downhill again to Graham Hill Bend, and along the short Cooper Straight behind the main paddock area, before the track goes sharply uphill and left at Surtees before the dip at Pilgrim's, Hawthorn Bend, and the Derek Minter Straight. The right-handed Westfield leads into yet another dip at Dingle Dell, followed by Sheene Curve and then Stirling's Bend, and on down to Clearways, Clark Curve, and finally back on to the Brabham Straight for the finish.

Between 1964 and 1986, the circuit hosted 12 British Grand Prix as well as the European Grand Prix in 1983 and 1985. Though no Grand Prixs have been held at Brands Hatch since, it remains the home of numerous top class racing events.

>>>>

Right: Riccardo Patrese (Brabham BT52B BMW) leads the field through Paddock Hill Bend at the start of the 1983 British and European Grand Prix at Brands Hatch.

BRANDS HATCH

TYPE:	purpose-built parkland
LOCATION:	Brands Hatch, England
CIRCUIT LENGTH:	2.60 miles (4.18 km)
LAP RECORD:	1:09.593
	(N Mansell/Williams-Honda 1986)

Druids Hill Bend, Brands Hatch at the start of the FIA Masters Historic Formula One Championship race May 27, 2013.

Caesar's Palace

CAESAR'S PALACE

<<< **Left:** Alan Jones (Williams FW07C Ford) leads going into Turn 1 on the first lap of the 1981 Caesar's Palace Grand Prix.

Money and Formula One go together like the proverbial horse and carriage, which was why the Grand Prix circus headed to Las Vegas after the contract to run the United States Grand Prix at Watkins Glen had expired.

From scratch, a 2.26 mile (3.64 km) circuit running in a counter-clockwise direction was built in Ceasar's Palace car park and yet there was so much space available that most drivers said that despite the debilitating effect of the desert sun, they enjoyed the venue because it left them plenty of space for overtaking. For safety's sake, generous sand-filled run-off areas were provided to slow down cars unfortunate enough to slide off the mirror-like road

surface. In fact, there was so little grip that watching the drivers battle with their sliding cars added considerably to the thrill of the event. And since spectators could get very close to the action, it was an unrivaled opportunity to catch the excitement of Grand Prix racing at close quarters.

Only two Formula One Championship races were held at Las Vegas, in 1981 and 1982, though two further non-championship events were held in 1983 and 1984. After that, Las Vegas returned to its roots as America's leading vacation and gambling resort.

CAESAR'S PALACE

TYPE:	city center car park
LOCATION:	Las Vegas, United States
CIRCUIT LENGTH:	2.26 miles (3.64 km)
LAP RECORD:	1:19.639 (M Alboreto/Tyrrell-Cosworth1982)

Canadian Grand Prix

CIRCUIT GILLES VILLENEUVE

Circuit Gilles Villeneuve is named after the French-Canadian superstar who was tragically killed in an accident while qualifying his Ferrari at the Zolder Circuit in Belgium. It is held on a man-made island in the St Lawrence River, on the site originally constructed for the 1976 Montreal Olympics.

The Canadian Grand Prix has been held in the city of Montreal since 1978; despite the fact that the circuit was purpose-designed, in many ways it has the atmosphere of a street circuit, partly because of its limited run-off areas and partly due to the majestic backdrop of the skyscrapers of downtown Montreal. Circuit Gilles Villeneuve is faster than any street circuit and its 2.71 mile (4.36 km) lap is a constant challenge to the teams and their drivers.

There are 15 corners in total, of which six are chicane-type complexes. There is also a long and very fast straight running from the Virage Du Casino to the start/finish area, which provides one of the most enthralling hard braking and tight turn-in sections, at its pit-lane entrance end. Here, drivers "kiss the wall" at the exit, getting as close as possible to the unyielding concrete that bears the legend "Bienvenue au Quebec."

Below: Jean Alesi (Ferrari 412T2) on the way to his maiden Grand Prix win at the 1995 Canadian Grand Prix at the Circuit Gilles Villenueve.

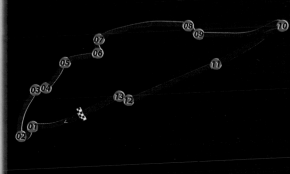

CIRCUIT GILLES VILLENEUVE

TYPE:	purpose-built city
LOCATION:	Montreal, Canada
CIRCUIT LENGTH:	2.71 miles (4.36 km)
LAP RECORD:	1:13.622
	(R Barrichello/Ferrari 2004)

0002234.56
450.4
9834568.23
44567.343
366585

Mark Webber, Red Bull Racing at the Formula 1 Canadian Grand
Prix in Montreal, Canada on Saturday, June 9, 2012.

Chinese Grand Prix

SHANGHAI INTERNATIONAL CIRCUIT

Claimed to be the most advanced Grand Prix
track in the world, the Shanghai International
Circuit was built from scratch on reclaimed
swampland and completed in May 2004 at a cost
of some $450 million.

The circuit itself can accommodate up to 200,000 people
and is characterized by its distinctive main buildings, which
bridge the track at either end of the start/finish area and
give diners in the splendid Sky Restaurant a unique view of
the racing below.

The challenging 3.37 mile (5.42 km) circuit has 16 turns,
interspersed by two long straights. The first three turns
occur in quick succession after the start/finish area,
followed by a fourth that opens out into a faster stretch
punctuated by the gentle kink of Turn 5. After the extended
hairpin of Turn 6, the track opens out again briefly for the
gentler Turns 7 and 8. Then it closes up again for Turns
9 and 10, before the short straight that precedes the
slower, more difficult Turns 11, 12, and 13. This
complex is followed by one of the longest straights
in Formula One, culminating in the tortuous right
hairpin of Turn 14, another kink right and then
the 90-degree left-hand turn into the start/
finish area. The Shanghai International
Circuit has quickly become a favorite
with drivers and spectators.

>>>

Right: Lewis Hamilton (McLaren MP4-23
Mercedes)—finished first—leads Kimi Räikkönen
(Ferrari F2008)—finished third—and Felipe Massa
(Ferrari F2008)—finished second—during the
2008 Chinese Grand Prix.

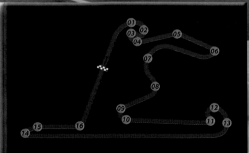

⚪ SHANGHAI INTERNATIONAL CIRCUIT

TYPE:	purpose-built
LOCATION:	Shanghai, China
CIRCUIT LENGTH:	3.37 miles (5.42 km)
LAP RECORD:	1:32.238
	(M Schumacher/Ferrari 2004)

0002234.56
450.4
99834568.2
44567.34
366585
35657686.57

Jenson Button of Great Britain, McLaren during the Chinese Formula One Grand Prix at the Shanghai International Circuit on April 14, 2013.

F1

Dutch Grand Prix

CIRCUIT PARK ZANDVOORT

The spectacular dune-peppered Circuit Park
Zandvoort, traditional home of the Dutch
Grand Prix, upholds the long-held belief in
motor racing circles that rural racing circuits
should not only follow the contours of the land
but also embrace natural hazards.

CIRCUIT PARK ZANDVOORT

TYPE:	purpose-built seaside
LOCATION:	15 miles (24 km) west of Amsterdam, Netherlands
CIRCUIT LENGTH:	2.63 miles (4.23 km)
LAP RECORD:	1:16.538 (A Prost/McLaren-TAG 1985)

42

Certainly, there were times at Zandvoort when the occasional sandstorm made life more difficult for drivers, but such freak occurrences could do nothing to dampen the enthusiasm of the spectators who lined the undulating 2.63 mile (4.23 km) track. A Grand Prix was held there almost every year from 1952 until the last Formula One race in 1985 (the only gaps being 1955–57 and 1972). It was much missed by drivers.

Zandvoort has many good vantage points; and the highest dune in the center of the track offers an almost clear view of every turn. Some of these bends carry names that long ago found their way into motor racing history, including Scheivlak Corner and the Tarzan Hairpin at the end of the pit straight. Just as interesting for the spectator was the exceptionally fast back stretch, which was later ruined by the installation of a chicane. The circuit includes a total of 14 bends of varying severity, a lightly wooded section, and, of course, the dunes themselves. It remains open, and rounds of various European motorsport championships are held there to this day.

<<<

Left: Alain Prost and Rene Arnoux (both Renault RE30Bs), lead Didier Pironi and Patrick Tambay (both Ferrari 126C2s) at the start of the 1982 Dutch Grand Prix.

0002234.56
450.4
99834568.23
44567.343
366585
35657686.575

French Grand Prix

PAUL RICARD

The Circuit Paul Ricard was founded in 1969 by the French drinks magnate of the same name. The original track was 3.6 miles (5.79 km) in length and was generally felt to be one of the safest in the world until the popular Italian driver Elio de Angelis was killed there after a crash during practice for the 1986 French Grand Prix. This led to a number of safety modifications and the last five Grand Prix to be held at the Paul Ricard (between 1986 and 1990) took place over the shortened 2.36 miles (3.8 km) circuit.

The Paul Ricard track ran in a clockwise direction, starting with the start/finish straight running alongside the pit lane, followed by a fast left-right kink at Verrière. A short straight ended in a right-left-right chicane followed by a further short straight before the double-apex right-hand bend at Saint Beaurne. Next came the challenging left-hand bend at L'école and the start of the Mistral Straight, which was punctuated by a chicane partway along its length. The track continued through the sweeping right-hander at Signes, followed by another short straight that ended in the tightening right-hand curve of Beausset. Then came a final complex of four bends—Bendor, Village, Tour, and the hairpin Virage du Pont—which lead back to the fast finishing straight.

The circuit is now known as the Paul Ricard High-Tech Test Track. The popular Provence circuit now includes a track-drenching facility and state-of-the art run-off areas.

● PAUL RICARD	
TYPE:	permanent circuit
LOCATION:	Le Castellet, France
CIRCUIT LENGTH:	3.6 miles (5.79 km) up to 1985; 2.36 miles (3.8 km) 1986–90
LAP RECORD:	1:39.914 (K Rosberg/Williams-Honda 1985)

French Grand Prix

MAGNY-COURS CIRCUIT

The Circuit de Nevers Magny-Cours, the track that has hosted the race more times than any other, remains one of the most controversial choices of venue in the calendar—not least because it is heartily disliked by most competitors as well as spectators.

The 2009 season marked the circuit's 50th anniversary. The French Grand Prix duly moved to Magny-Cours in 1991. Magny-Cours was always a very quick track, with a typical lap starting on the wide start/finish straight leading into the fast left-handed Grande Courbe. After another short straight, a slight left led up to the medium-speed Estoril right-hand bend; then on to the back straight, which featured the fast kink right at Golf half way.

The highly challenging Adelaide Hairpin was the scene of countless indiscretions as drivers struggled under hard braking to find the best line through the bend to the right. The next section comprised the fast Nürburgring right hand bend, followed by an equally fast left-hand curve to the turn known as "180" with its difficult tightening exit. Then came the Imola Complex of right and left hand bends, followed by the tight-right Chateau d'Eaubend, a straight leading to another right-handed bend at Lycée then through to the start/finish line.

Below: Nelson Piquet Jr. (Renault R28) leads Lewis Hamilton (McLaren MP4-23 Mercedes) during the 2008 French Grand Prix at Magny-Cours.

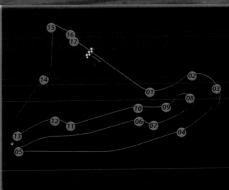

MAGNY-COURS CIRCUIT

TYPE:	permanent circuit
LOCATION:	10 miles (16 km) south of Nevers, France
CIRCUIT LENGTH:	2.4 miles (3.86 km) 1971–91;
	2.63 (4.23 km) 1992–2002;
	2.73 miles (4.39 km) 2003–08
LAP RECORD:	1:15.377 (M Schumacher/Ferrari 2004)

Mauricio Gugelmin (March CG891 Judd) is involved in a huge crash at the start of the 1989 French Grand Prix at Circuit Paul Ricard.

German Grand Prix

HOCKENHEIMRING

The Hockenheimring is a superb venue for both drivers and spectators alike. It has always been notoriously fast, claiming the lives of Jim Clark in a Formula Two race in 1968 and Formula One driver Patrick Depailler in 1980. New chicanes were later added at the locations of both fatal crashes in an effort to cut speeds and make the circuit safer for the drivers.

Hockenheim remains first and foremost a multi-discipline motorsports circuit, and during an average season plays host to everything from single-seat formulae, classic, sports, and touring car racing to drifting championships and drag racing.

From the start/finish area near the pits, drivers first of all have to contend with the fast right Nordkurve and a short straight before reaching the tight right-hander and extended fast left that leads to the sweeping Parabolika curve. Following this, a right-hand hairpin leads to a short back straight, after which a right-left-right series of corners leads to another short straight. The track then turns right at the Mobil 1 curve into the stadium complex, which incorporates the famous Sachs hairpin. One last left-right-right series of bends before the Südkurve completes the lap.

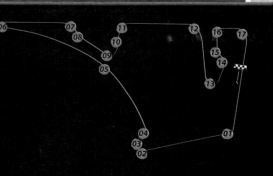

Below: Rene Arnoux and Alain Prost (both Renault RE30Bs) lead the field away at the start of the 1982 German Grand Prix at Hockenheim.

⬤ HOCKENHEIMRING

TYPE:	permanent circuit
LOCATION:	15 miles (24 km) west of Heidelberg, Germany
CIRCUIT LENGTH:	2.83 miles (4.55 km)
LAP RECORD:	1:13.780 (K Raikkonen/ McLaren-Mercedes 2004)

German Grand Prix

NÜRBURGRING

Few Grand Prix venues in the motor racing world possess more charisma than the Nürburgring, located amid the spectacular scenery of the Eifel Mountains in western Germany. It is still used today as a racing circuit and, unusually, it's also open to the public who can pay by the lap to drive their own cars on the famous track.

It has hosted the German and European Grand Prix from time to time and also the Luxembourg Grand Prix in 1997 and 98 as well as many other sporting events including single-seater formulae, motorcycle and 24-hour endurance racing, sports car and saloon racing, and even truck racing.

The Nürburgring is also used by the world's leading car makers as a proving ground for their performance cars, and several manufacturers maintain permanent technical facilities nearby, not least because there is enormous competition surrounding the fastest lap time by a production car.

While the original Nordschleife circuit contains some of the most famous-name bends in motor racing history—the Flugplatz, Karusell, Hohe Acht, and Pflanzgarten—even the shortened Grand Prix circuit contains some of the fastest and most difficult bends in the current Formula One calendar. The only real overtaking opportunities are at the highly-demanding Castrol S-Bend at the end of the start/finish straight and Veedol-Schikane which comes on the run down one of the fastest downhill sections in the world.

Below: Mike Hawthorn (Lancia-Ferrari D50) leads Juan Manuel Fangio (Maserati 250F) in the closing laps of the 1957 Grand Prix at Nürburgring. Fangio later passed Hawthorn to win his greatest race.

● NÜRBURGRING

TYPE:	permanent circuit
LOCATION:	village of Nürburg, west of Bonn, Germany
CIRCUIT LENGTH:	3.20 miles (5.15 km)
LAP RECORD:	1:29.468 (M Schumacher/Ferrari 2004)

Fernando Alonso of Spain, Ferrari on his way to winning the German Grand Prix at Hockenheimring on July 22, 2012.

Hungarian *Grand Prix*

HUNGARORING

The Hungaroring at Mogyoród near Budapest made its debut as a Grand Prix circuit in 1986. Known locally as the "Shallow Plate," its location in a valley surrounded by rolling countryside creates a natural viewing bowl for spectators and it means that the vast majority of the action can be seen from any one point around the circuit.

With 16 bends ranging in radius from around 20 yards (18 meters) to 400 yards (370 meters), the Hungaroring presents plenty of overtaking opportunities. At almost exactly 1 km (0.62 miles) in length, the start/finish straight is also long enough for most Formula One cars to reach speeds of around 200 mph (320 kph), before going hard on the brakes for the following hairpin bend.

Drivers progress through another fast stretch toward a sharp left turn that doubles back into a right-left-right hairpin and the first of two back straights. A kink to the right at the end is followed abruptly by a turn to the left and a sweeping right-hander leading to the right-left hairpin of turns 8 and 9. Sharp left and right turns break up the otherwise fast back section, which ends in a 90-degree right-hander that precedes the second straight. Then comes a loop, crowned by a fairly tight 180-degree left-hand turn, before the slightly quicker right-hander that returns the driver to the flat-out start/finish straight.

Below: Heikki Kovalainen (McLaren MP4-23 Mercedes)—who won the race—leads Nico Rosberg (Williams FW30 Toyota) during the 2008 Hungarian Grand Prix.

v v v
v v v
v

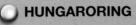

⬤ **HUNGARORING**

TYPE:	permanent circuit
LOCATION:	12.5 miles (20 km) northeast of Budapest, Hungary
CIRCUIT LENGTH:	2.72 miles (4.38 km)
LAP RECORD:	1:19.071 (M Schumacher/Ferrari 2004)

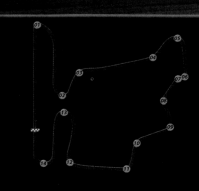

0002234.56
450.4
99834568.23
44567.343
366585
35657686 575

Indian Grand Prix

BUDDH INTERNATIONAL CIRCUIT

Originally announced that it would debut in Formula One for 2009, then postponed to 2010, India finally launched its Formula One track in the 2011 season with Sebastian Vettel winning and achieving the fastest time in the very last lap. In 2012, with Red Bull, he went on to win again, with Alonso and Webber coming 2nd and 3rd.

The Buddh International Circuit is part of a large sports development set in 2,500 acres (10 km²) containing an international cricket stadium, golf course, hockey stadium and a sports academy. When the racetrack was designed, all Formula One teams were given copies of the design and asked for feedback on how it could be improved to aid overtaking. The result of this consultation was that a hairpin at Turn 7 was removed and the track at Turn 3 was widened.

One of the most notable sections of the circuit is the multi-apex Turn 10–11–12 sequence which has been compared to the long, fast Turn 8 at Turkey's Istanbul Park Circuit.

The 600m pit lane is one of the longest in Formula One and has to be massively factored into the race strategy of the teams.

From the start there is a bit of length before hitting the slow, tight right-hand Turn 1. Exiting the turn, there is an uphill, full-throttle before going into left-hand Turn 2.

Turn 3 is another slow right-hand turn leading into the straight, which is quite long with a beautiful elevation profile. Turn 4 is an overtaking turn to the right. Then another straight with a short braking zone into a quick left-hand Turn 5, immediately followed by a tight left turn into a right turn.

A chicane of a right-hand Turn 8 is followed by a left-hand 9 and an uphill straight into a long right Turn 10–11–12. Coming out of this turn is a downhill run preceding a connected pair of left and right Turns 13 and 14 with a fast exit and an uphill straight into a right-hand Turn 15, which gives overtaking possibilities before going downhill into the final corner with a tight pit entrance on the left.

BUDDH INTERNATIONAL CIRCUIT

TYPE:	permanent circuit
LOCATION:	Noida, New Delhi
CIRCUIT LENGTH:	3.19 miles (5.14 km)
LAP RECORD:	1:27.249 (Sebastian Vettel/Red Bull 2011)

Below: Adrian Sutil of Germany and Force India drives during the Indian Formula One Grand Prix at the Buddh International Circuit on October 30, 2011 in Noida.

V V V
 V V
  V

Felipe Massa of Brazil, Ferrari leads from Lewis Hamilton of Great Britain, McLaren during the Indian Formula One Grand Prix at the Buddh International Circuit on October 30, 2011 in Noida.

Italian Grand Prix

AUTODROMO NAZIONALE MONZA

The Autodromo Nazionale di Monza, located within a park to the north of the city of the same name, is the most famous motor racing circuit in Italy and one of the best-known in the world.

Monza's circuit was always a high-speed layout that incorporated both a 3.4 mile (5.5 km) road track and a 2.8 mile (4.5 km) oval with banked sections that boosted top speeds without unduly compromising safety. The original Grand Prix road track has remained largely unaltered for most of its existence.

In common with other famous motor racing venues, Monza's corners have become famous throughout the world. They include the Variante del Rettifilo, the tight chicane that's the first hazard the drivers meet after the start of the race. This is followed by the fast Curva Grande and yet another chicane at Variante della Roggia. A short straight is then followed by the challenging double right-handed Curve di Lesmo, which in turn leads onto the equally challenging Curva del Serraglio. From here, there's a short straight under the original banked oval and into the fast Variante Ascari chicane. This is followed by another short straight and finally into the long right-handed 180-degree Curva Parabolica that leads back to the start/finish straight.

Right: Michael Schumacher >>>> (Ferrari 248F1) in the lead during the 2006 Italian Grand Prix at Monza.

AUTODROMO NAZIONALE MONZA

TYPE:	permanent circuit
LOCATION:	9.3 miles (15 km) northeast of Milan, Italy
CIRCUIT LENGTH:	3.59 miles (5.78 km)
LAP RECORD:	1:21.046 (R Barrichello/Ferrari 2004)

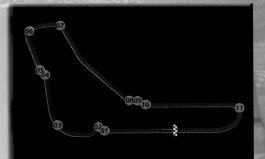

Fernando Alonso in a Ferrari F10 races in the Italian Grand Prix, on September 11, 2010 in Monza, Italy.

*J*apanese *Grand Prix*

SUZUKA CIRCUIT

Suzuka International Racing Course is one of the few circuits in the world to employ a figure-of-eight crossover layout. At a total length of 3.6 miles (5.80 km), its intricate and highly technical layout offers a considerable challenge for drivers: in particular, the changes in elevation create a number of blind bends where judging the exit can be difficult.

Below: Fernando Alonso (Renault R26) passes Ralf Schumacher (Toyota TF106B) on his way to winning the 2006 Japanese Grand Prix at Suzuka.

⬤ SUZUKA CIRCUIT

TYPE:	permanent circuit
LOCATION:	Suzuka City, Japan
CIRCUIT LENGTH:	3.6 miles (5.80 km)
LAP RECORD:	1:31.540
	(K Räikkönen/McLaren 2005)

A lap of the track commences one-third of the way up the start/finish straight, which leads into the extended right-handed hairpin of Turn 1—also known as First. After a short straight comes a sequence of five bends, culminating in the fast Dunlop left-hander which leads into the mid-speed right at Degner and a tighter right at Turn 9. The circuit then ducks under the crossover bridge to the fast right-hander at Turn 10, followed by the sharply left-handed Hairpin. Drivers continue through another double-apex right-hander and on to the very fast Spoon—an extended left-hander that leads to the Crossover, the fastest stretch of the track. This is followed by the incredibly challenging left-handed 130R, which has undergone extensive modification following serious accidents in 2002 and 2003. Finally, it's into the Casio Triangle, three corners numbered 15, 16, and 17, which effectively meld into one long right hander that opens onto the start of the finishing straight.

0002234.56
450.4
99834568.23
44567.343
366585
35657686.575

Adrian Sutil of Force India-Mercedes during free practice at 2011 Formula 1 Japanese Grand Prix on October 7, 2011 in Suzuka, Japan.

Korean Grand Prix

KOREA INTERNATIONAL CIRCUIT

Despite military tensions within Korea, in 2010 Formula One debuted at the Korea International Circuit in South Korea. It was welcomed into the Formula One family after a deal between Bernie Ecclestone and Korean Formula One promoter Auto Valley Operation.

One of the most recognized and respected track designers, Hermann Tilke from Germany, was engaged in 2009 to design the track. He created a part-permanent and part-temporary track along the harbor front, with some of the city streets being used for the pit lane. Finishing the construction on time proved to be a very close-run thing, with Korea missing the FIA technical inspection scheduled for 28th September 2010, despite announcing at the end of 2009 that everything was on track. This inspection is crucial, as a Formula One license can only be awarded once the inspection is passed. In the event, the two-day inspection took place 11 days before the first practice sessions were due to start and the license was issued through the Korea Automobile Racing Association.

The circuit starts with a double left hander; the first corner is taken in second gear, with the drivers accelerating through the second turn. This opens up onto a 0.75 miles (1.2 km) straight – the longest on a circuit in Asia – which in turn feeds into the slowest corner on the circuit, a second-gear right-hand bend. The cars follow a shorter straight, home to the support pits, before a series of tight switchbacks at Turns 4, 5 and 6; all three are taken in second gear. The circuit then opens up again, flowing through a series of fast fifth-gear bends, before the driver must brake for Turn 10, a tight right-hander whose approach is made more difficult by the position of the braking zone on a downward-sloping incline. The remainder of the circuit is modeled on a street circuit, and follows a labyrinth series of left and right-hand bends that lead to Turn 17, a long right-hander that is completely blind as it is surrounded by walls. The final turn on the circuit is a left-hand kink that feeds onto the main straight.

Below: Atmosphere during the Korean Formula One Grand Prix at the Korea International Circuit on October 14, 2012.

KOREA INTERNATIONAL CIRCUIT

TYPE:	part temporary, part permanent circuit
LOCATION:	Yeongham, 250 miles (400 km) south of Seoul
CIRCUIT LENGTH:	3.49 miles (5.62 km)
LAP RECORD:	1:39.605 (Sebastian Vettel/Red Bull 2011)

The pit lane has been one of the most contested features of the Korea International Circuit. In 2010, drivers criticized placing the entry on the racing line exit of a corner that is taken at speeds in excess of 150 mph. This meant that those pitting would be driving dangerously slow on the racing line. The pit lane exit has also been criticized as it feeds into the outside of Turn 1. In 2011, Nico Rosberg, Mercedes, locked up at the turn and ran wide, colliding with Jaime Alguersuari, Toro Rosso, although that particular incident didn't actually occur on the racing line.

Top: Start of the Korean Formula One Grand Prix at the Korea International Circuit.

Sebastian Vettel of Germany, Red Bull Racing drives in for a pit stop on his way to finishing second during the Korean Formula One Grand Prix at the Korea International Circuit on October 14, 2012.

Malaysian Grand Prix

SEPANG INTERNATIONAL CIRCUIT

Built on the site of a former palm oil plantation, the Sepang International Circuit was completed in a record 14 months and was opened on March 9, 1999, by the Prime Minister of Malaysia.

Sepang's astonishing facilities include an enormous three-storey Pit Building which, as well as the 33 pits, contains all the management offices and officials' quarters. Next door is the Welcome Building which boasts shops, restaurants, and an exhibition center. On the other side of the Pit Building is a Medical Center that can be converted in an emergency into a fully-equipped hospital, complete with operating theaters.

The centrally located main grandstands guarantee fantastic views of the action, and can seat 32,000 people as well as accommodating various corporate entertainment suites.

At just under 3.5 miles (5.54 km) long, the full Sepang Grand Prix circuit contains 15 turns and eight straights, which means some of the highest top speeds in Formula One are seen here. The width of the track also offers plenty of overtaking opportunities. The unique parallel configuration of the start/finish and back straights, with just a single hairpin in between them, allows the track to be divided into North and South circuits for smaller events, such as kart racing.

>>>>>

Right: Felipe Massa (Ferrari F2008) leads the field at the start of the 2008 Malaysian Grand Prix.

⬤ SEPANG INTERNATIONAL CIRCUIT

TYPE:	permanent circuit
LOCATION:	Kuala Lumpur, Malaysia
CIRCUIT LENGTH:	3.44 miles (5.54 km)
LAP RECORD:	1:34.223 (J P Montoya/Williams-BMW 2004)

0002234.56
450.4
99834568.23
44567.343
366585
35657686.575

Nico Rosberg of Germany, Mercedes Team at top speed on the
main straight at the Malaysian Formula 1 Grand Prix April 4, 2010.

Mexican Grand Prix

AUTÓDROMO HERMANOS RODRÍGUEZ

Left: Jo Siffert (Lotus 49B-Ford Cosworth) follows through The Esses on the opening lap of the 1968 Mexican Grand Prix.

<<<<

The Magdalena Mixhuca Circuit in the heart of Mexico City hosted its first non-Championship Formula One event in 1962, the year of its opening. A further 14 races were held there up until 1970, followed by another run from 1986 to 1992. In 1980, the tragic death of the second Rodriguez brother, Pedro, led to the circuit being renamed the Autódromo Hermanos Rodriguez in their honor.

There have been several rumors that Grand Prix racing will return to the venue, but so far none of them has materialized.

In its heyday the circuit could be configured in a number of ways, even as an oval for stock car racing. The Grand Prix track consisted of a long start/finish straight which lead into an extremely difficult series of bends which exited onto another straight. Drivers were then faced with another awkward complex of 10 bends one after the other that finally ended on part of the oval track, after which they doubled back to the finishing line, about a third of the way down the start/finish straight. The already considerable challenges of the circuit were increased in the early days by rowdy spectators: there was severe overcrowding at some of the corners, and too often spectators moved onto the track to gain a better view of the action.

⬤ AUTÓDROMO HERMANOS RODRÍGUEZ

TYPE:	permanent circuit
LOCATION:	Mexico City, Mexico
CIRCUIT LENGTH:	2.75 miles (4.42 km)
LAP RECORD:	1:16.788
	(N Mansell/Williams-Renault 1991)

Monaco Grand Prix

CIRCUIT DE MONACO

By rights, the Grand Prix de Monaco—held on the narrow streets of the tiny Principality—should not exist: at just over 2 miles (3.22 km) in length, the circuit is theoretically too confined for the demands of Formula One. Yet anyone trying to find a word said against this magical venue will struggle, for Monaco truly embraces the spirit of Grand Prix motor racing.

The basic layout of the circuit was established, with the start/finish line on the road above the harbor, followed by a tight right at Sainte Devote, then up the hill and left into Casino Square. On the exit of the Square the road switches downhill to the Mirabeau corner, followed by the ultra-slow Lowe's Hairpin (named for the famous hotel, which later became The Grand). Then it's into the long, slightly right-hand curved tunnel before emerging back into the sunshine for the chicane at the harbor side, followed by the tricky swimming pool section. Finally, it's down to the right-hand final bend at the Gasometer (later to become known as Rascasse) and back into the start/finish straight.

Overtaking opportunities at Monaco are minimal, and the high curbs and roadside walls present a constant threat to drivers who stray off-line. The racing is always eventful at Monaco, and it remains the jewel of the Formula One calendar.

Right: Fernando Alonso (Renault R26) leads Michael Schumacher (Ferrari 248F1) during the 2006 Monaco Grand Prix: Alonso went on to win the race.

CIRCUIT DE MONACO

TYPE:	street circuit
LOCATION:	Monte Carlo, Monaco
CIRCUIT LENGTH:	2.07 miles (3.34 km)
LAP RECORD:	1:14.439 (M Schumacher/Ferrari 2004)

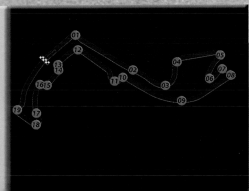

Lewis Hamilton (McLaren MP4-23 Mercedes) negotiates the wrecked car of Nico Rosberg (Williams FW30 Toyota) on his way to winning the 2008 Monaco Grand Prix.

CÉDEZ LE PASSAGE

Moroccan Grand Prix

AIN-DIAB

Moroccan interest in motor racing dates back to 1925, when a Grand Prix was held in the Atlantic coastal city of Casablanca during the days when the nation was still a French dependency.

Formula One motor racing returned to Morocco in 1954 at a sports car circuit in the southern coastal resort of Agadir, where it remained for two years. But in 1957 came the Suez Crisis, which threatened to play havoc with the Grand Prix calendar due to the fuel shortages and transportation difficulties which resulted from the closure of the Suez Canal. Seizing what he perceived as a golden opportunity to supplant one of the big European Grand Prix, Sultan Mohammed V ordered the hasty construction of the Ain-Diab Street Circuit in Casablanca—a project that was completed in just six weeks.

The following year, an officially sanctioned Grand Prix did take place on the dusty Ain-Diab track and was won by Englishman Stirling Moss driving a Vanwall. Sadly, the event was marred by the horrific crash of Moss's team-mate Stuart Lewis-Evans, whose engine seized (reputedly due to the dust) and sent him plunging into the barriers, his car in flames. His death cast a shadow over the Grand Prix, which saw the Formula One circus abandon Morocco, never to return.

Above: Stirling Moss (Vanwall VW5) during his winning drive at the 1958 Moroccan Grand Prix.

AIN-DIAB

TYPE:	street circuit
LOCATION:	Ain-Diab, Morocco
CIRCUIT LENGTH:	4.75 miles (7.64 km)
LAP RECORD:	2:22.500 (S Moss/Vanwall 1958)

Portuguese Grand Prix

AUTÓDROMO DO ESTORIL

Built in Estoril, the seaside resort near Lisbon, the new Autódromo do Estoril soon became a favorite with drivers thanks to its elevation changes and its tight and difficult nature.

After hosting many junior formulae and Formula Two European Championship races during the 1970s, a total of 13 Grand Prix were held there between 1984 and 1996. Following the deaths of Ayrton Senna and Austrian driver Roland Ratzenburger at Imola in 1994, the circuit's organizers became increasingly preoccupied with safety. The 2.72 mile (4.38 km) layout was modified to replace the very fast Tanque Corner with a much slower complex of corners known collectively as Gancho, and the Parabolica bend leading on to the start/finish straight was renamed in Senna's honor.

Although Grand Prix racing continued at Estoril for another three seasons, it became clear that even in its modified form, the circuit was simply too dangerous for the latest generation of Formula One cars. It did continue hosting major events including the FAI GT Championships, the DTM series, and more recently a round of the A1 Grand Prix and even the Portuguese Motorcycle Grand Prix. Estoril was suggested as the venue for the 1997 European Grand Prix, but in the end it was decided it could not reach the required safety standards so the idea was dropped.

Below: Rubens Barrichello (Jordan 195 Peugeot) leads Mika Häkkinen and Mark Blundell (both McLaren MP4/10B Mercedes) during the 1995 Portuguese Grand Prix at Estoril.

⬤ AUTÓDROMO DO ESTORIL

TYPE:	permanent circuit
LOCATION:	Estoril, Portugal
CIRCUIT LENGTH:	2.72 miles (4.38 km)
LAP RECORD:	1:22.446
	(D Coulthard/Williams-Renault 1994)

San Marino Grand Prix

AUTODROMO ENZO E DINO FERRARI

The Imola circuit, in the foothills of the Apennine Mountains, was opened in 1952, although the nearby parkland had been used for motocross races for some years before. But it would not be until 1963 that the first Grand Prix was held at the circuit, a non-Championship event that was won by Scots driver Jim Clark in a Lotus-Climax.

The track was at first named for the Santerno River which runs alongside it, but Imola was officially renamed the Autodromo Enzo e Dino Ferrari after the death of Enzo Ferrari and his son Dino.

The circuit has been changed many times over the years, most notably by the addition of three chicanes—the Variante Bassa in 1973, the Variante Alta in 1974, and the Acque Minerale in 1981—to slow cars down. There have also been alterations to the very fast Tamburello corner, the scene of many terrifying accidents over the years, not least the one in 1994 that killed Ayrton Senna. Villeneuve Corner, where Roland Ratzenberger was killed, was also modified after that year's tragic events. The last Formula One race was held at Imola in 2006, and while motor racing continues at the venue, it remains to be seen if Formula One will ever return.

Above:
Fernando Alonso (Renault R26) during a pitstop at the 2006 San Marino Grand Prix.

<< **Left:**
Michael Schumacher (Ferrari 248F1) leads Jenson Button (HondaRA106) early in the 2006 San Marino Grand Prix. Schumacher went on to win the race.

⬤ AUTODROMO ENZO E DINO FERRARI

TYPE:	permanent circuit
LOCATION:	Imola, 25 miles (40 km) east of Bologna, Italy
CIRCUIT LENGTH:	3.06 miles (4.93 km)
LAP RECORD:	1:20.411 (M Schumacher/Ferrari 2004)

Singapore Grand Prix

MARINA BAY STREET CIRCUIT

The 'new' Singapore Grand Prix was first held in 2008 on a 3.15 mile (5.07 km) circuit created on public roads in the Marina Bay suburb of the city. Memorable for being held at night, the race took place against a stunning vista of illuminated skyscrapers and provided a thrilling spectacle for all who watched it.

The 2008 Formula One race was the result of a $150 million ($103 million) deal signed by the FIA, the Singapore government, and Singapore Telecommunications, and was run in a counter-clockwise direction on a circuit consisting of no less than 10 right-hand and 14 left-hand turns. Lap times came down quickly as drivers got used to the night-time conditions, but the use of hi-tech projectors to illuminate the track ensured that the race ran smoothly—despite a number of collisions against the high curbs at Turn 10.

The event, which was eventually won by Fernando Alonso in a Renault, was also a huge commercial success, with around 110,000 tickets sold and all of the corporate hospitality suites sold out. The Malaysian Grand Prix in Kuala Lumpur is staged only 180 miles (290 km) away, but the evident popularity of Formula One in this part of the world suggests that there is room for both to thrive.

Right: Fernando Alonso (Renault R28) on his way to winning the 2008 Singapore Grand Prix. >>>>

⬤ MARINA BAY STREET CIRCUIT

TYPE:	street circuit
LOCATION:	Marina Bay, Singapore
CIRCUIT LENGTH:	3.15 miles (5.07 km)
LAP RECORD:	1:45.599
	(K Raikkonen/Ferrari 2008)

0002234.567
450.45
99834568.234
44567.3434
3665854
35657686.575

Fernando Alonso (Renault R26) during a pitstop at the 2006 San Marino Grand Prix.

South African Grand Prix

KYALAMI CIRCUIT

The Kyalami Circuit hosted the South African Grand Prix 20 times between 1967 and 1993 and would probably have staged more had it not been for an international boycott during the Apartheid years of 1986 to 1991.

Kyalami in Zulu, one of South Africa's 11 languages, means 'my home', and since it first opened in 1961 it has welcomed many different race series to Johannesburg. Today's circuit is very different to the original that was in use from 1967 to 1985. Then, it was 2.55 miles (4.1 km) long and one of the fastest circuits on the calendar. It had a long main straight, punctuated by The Kink and then the very challenging Crowthorne Corner and Barbeque Bend. Then another long sweep up to Sunset Bend, a tough left Clubhouse Bend, then left again into The

Esses, before the long Leeukop bend back onto the start/finish straight. In 1985, while the Grand Prix was absent, Kyalami was radically revised and only a small section of the original track was retained. The new track with its smooth surface offered a variety of fast and slow corners and presented an interesting technical challenge to drivers. By this time it was slightly longer than before, at 2.66 miles (4.28 km).

Below: Ayrton Senna (McLaren MP4/8 Ford) leads Michael Schumacher (Benetton B192B Ford) during the 1993 South African Grand Prix at Kyalami.

KYALAMI CIRCUIT

TYPE:	permanent circuit
LOCATION:	Johannesburg, South Africa
CIRCUIT LENGTH:	2.66 miles (4.28 km)
LAP RECORD:	1:17.578 (N Mansell/Williams-Renault 1992)

0002234.56
450.4
99834568.23
44567.343
366585
35657686.575

Spanish Grand Prix

CIRCUIT DE CATALUNYA

Often referred to simply as "Barcelona," the Circuit de Catalunya near the town of Montmeló was opened on September 10, 1991 with strong backing of the Catalan Government and the Reial Automòbil Club de Catalunya (RACC). It will always be remembered for the the head-to-head duel between Nigel Mansell and Ayrton Senna that lasted the full length of the start/finish straight.

Catalunya Grand Prix track is characterized by its exceptionally long starting straight and 16 highly demanding turns; a typical lap starts with a lengthy burst down the starting straight, followed by a right turn at Elf Corner and then a fast left onto the extended Renault right-hander. The track then keeps right into the double-apex Repsol Bend, then straightens briefly before the slow Seat Bend. After this it dips to Wurth and climbs up again to the left-handed Campsa, before entering a fast downhill section that ends with the slow uphill left turn at Caixa. Drivers face an even stiffer test as they enter the Bank Sabadell complex of turns before passing through the fast right-hander at New Holland to return to the start/finish straight.

A much commented-on feature of the circuit is the wind, which can abruptly change direction during the day and throw the cars' sensitive aerodynamic set-ups into disarray.

Right: Kimi Räikkönen and Felipe Massa (both Ferrari F2008) lead the field at the start of the 2008 Spanish Grand Prix. >>>>

⬤ CIRCUIT DE CATALUNYA

TYPE:	permanent circuit
LOCATION:	13 miles (21 km) north of Barcelona, Spain
CIRCUIT LENGTH:	2.91 miles (4.65 km)
LAP RECORD:	1:21.670 (K Räikkönen/Ferrari 2008)

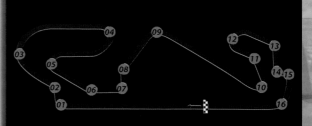

0002234.56
450.4
99834568.23
44567.343
366585
35657686.575

Sebastian Vettel of Germany, during a Formula
One Test Day at Circuit de Catalunya, Barcelona,
Spain February 21, 2012.

Swedish Grand Prix

SCANDINAVIAN RACEWAY

The Scandinavian Raceway was built 3 miles (5 km) east of Gislaved in Sweden in 1968; it is built on flat, marshy land in the middle of a forest and is an extremely fast circuit owing to its long straights.

A lap starts with a run down to the StartKurvan, a right-hand hairpin that leads into a short straight that finishes at the left-hand hairpin, Opel. The first of the circuit's straights leads to the left-handed Hansen Curve then it's down to the fast and challenging 180-degree right-turn at Karusell. Gislaved marks the end of the Karusell, then there's a short blast to the double-apex Södra which leads on to the longest straight. It's called the Flight Straight, not least because it doubles as a runway. At the end is the difficult right-handed Norra corner that leads to a brief straight and then another right-hander at Läktar that leads back on to the start/finish straight.

Six Formula One races were held at the Scandinavian Raceway between 1973 and 1978, with the first one prominently featuring local hero Ronnie Peterson.

The last Swedish Grand Prix at the Raceway was held in 1978, the year in which Swedes Gunnar Nilsson and Ronnie Peterson both died.

<<<< **Left:** Patrick Depailler (Tyrrell P34 Ford) during the 1976 Swedish Grand Prix. He finished in second position behind Jody Scheckter.

SCANDINAVIAN RACEWAY

TYPE:	permanent circuit
LOCATION:	Anderstorp, Sweden
CIRCUIT LENGTH:	2.5 miles (4.02 km)
LAP RECORD:	1:24.836
	(N Lauda/Brabham-Alfa Romeo 1978)

Swiss Grand Prix

BREMGARTEN

The Circuit Bremgarten, situated in an ancient forest near the city of Berne, hosted the Swiss Grand Prix between 1950 and 1954. The circuit was purpose-built for motor racing and the Grand Prix only stopped being held there following the tragic accident at Le Mans in 1955 which resulted in the authorities banning motor racing on Swiss soil.

Before that, Switzerland had been one of Europe's most enthusiastic motorsport countries, putting on numerous international car and motorcycle races over the years.

The circuit itself follows an oval shape and, unusually, there are no straights of any length throughout its 4.52 miles (7.27 km). It was a fast circuit and one which could be highly dangerous as it coursed through the trees, because of sudden changes of light and an inconsistent surface that was especially difficult in wet conditions.

The Grand Prix Bern got a new lease of life during the summer of 1998, when for a single day classic motorcyles returned for a parade event on the historic Bremgarten track. Later, in 2004, a similar event for cars was held and it is planned to continue the tradition every three years. An attempt to raise Switzerland's ban on motor racing was made in 2007 but it was not successful.

Above: Alan Brown (Cooper T20-Bristol) leads Stirling Moss (HWM 52-Alta), Emmanuel de Graffenried (Maserati 4CLT/48-Plate), George Abecassis (HWM 52-Alta), and Peter Collins (HWM 52-Alta) at the 1952 Swiss Grand Prix.

CIRCUIT BREMGARTEN

TYPE:	permanent parkland circuit
LOCATION:	Bremgarten, Berne, Switzerland
CIRCUIT LENGTH:	4.52 miles (7.27 km)
LAP RECORD:	2:39.700 (J M Fangio/Mercedes-Benz 1954)

Turkish Grand Prix

ISTANBUL PARK

The Istanbul track that hosts the Turkish Grand Prix was designed, as were so many other modern Grand Prix circuits, by Hermann Tilke. As well as having numerous changes of elevation, the track mirrors some of the most famous corners from other tracks around the world but also has one of its own that presents a unique challenge to Grand Prix drivers. It's called Turn 8 and it's a massively long left-handed bend with four separate apexes during which the cars are pulling up to 5G in cornering force.

This extremely challenging 3.31 mile (5.34 km) sinuous circuit runs counter-clockwise, making it, along with Brazil and Singapore, the only current Grand Prix circuit to do so. Unlike many Tilke circuits, there are no long straights followed by a tight bend or hairpin to provide overtaking opportunities. Instead, Istanbul's four different gradient changes and successions of technical corners make it easy for a driver under pressure to make mistakes, though the start/finish straight at almost half a mile (800 meters) in length permits speed of over 200 mph (322 kph) to be reached. There's plenty of variation in the width of the track, too, ranging from 18.5 to 26.5 yards (17 to 24.25 meters), and in all there are 14 corners.

>>>>

Right: Giancarlo Fisichella (Force India VJM01 Ferrari) slams into the back of Kazuki Nakajima (Williams FW30 Toyota) during the 2008 Turkish Grand Prix.

⦿ ISTANBUL PARK

TYPE:	permanent circuit
LOCATION:	Tuzla, Istanbul, Turkey
CIRCUIT LENGTH:	3.31 miles (5.34 km)
LAP RECORD:	1:24.770 (J Montoya/McLaren 2005)

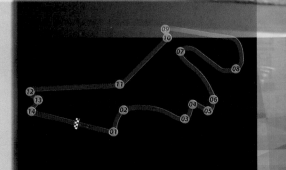

0002234.56?
450.4?
99834568.23?
44567.343?
366585?
35657686.575?

USA Grand Prix

PHOENIX STREET CIRCUIT

The United States Grand Prix was hosted three times on the streets of Phoenix, Arizona, between 1989 and 1991.

The biggest problem was faced by the drivers who had to contend with little grip, poor and inconsistent road surfaces, and a dull succession of blind 90-degree corners. Another problem was that the catch fencing required for safety was both ugly and restricted spectators' views. The first Phoenix Grand Prix was held in the searing heat of summer which not only took its toll on the drivers but also on the spectators, many of whom left early to seek cooling refreshment and shelter from the Arizona sun. The writing was on the wall and after the 1991 event, Formula One left Pheonix, Arizona.

The Phoenix Grand Prix was held downtown, its counter-clockwise circuit starting on Jefferson Street and taking in Monroe Street, Washington Street, 3rd Avenue, Adams Street, and 5th Avenue before a long double left-hand sequence to return to the start/finish straight. For 1991, however, the construction of the state baseball stadium, the Bank One Ballpark, meant the track changed course, to run along Madison Street after the start, with the Monroe Street loop being eliminated.

In 2012, the USA Grand Prix was revived in Travis County, Texas. Named the Circuit of the Americas, the inaugural race was the penultimate round of the 2012 championship. Lewis Hamilton won the race, with Sebastian Vettel coming second and Fernando Alonso third.

>>>>

Right: The 1989 United States Grand Prix in Phoenix, Arizona. Ayrton Senna leads Alain Prost (both McLaren MP4/5 Hondas) at the start.

● PHOENIX STREET CIRCUIT

TYPE:	street circuit
LOCATION:	Phoenix, Arizona, United States
CIRCUIT LENGTH:	2.32 miles (3.73 km)
LAP RECORD:	1:26.758 (J Alesi/Ferrari 1991)

0002234.567
450.45
99834568.234
44567.3439
3665854
35657686.575

Lewis Hamilton, Sebastian Vettel and Fernando Alonso celebrate in November 2012 after the United States Grand Prix was held in Travis County, Texas.

The Constructors

Soon after the motorcar was invented, people began to wonder how fast and how far they might be made to go. Reliability trials and actual races were soon commonplace. From that time onward, the standard offering from motor manufacturers would never be good enough, because to race ever faster required more and more specialized machinery.

At the beginning of the 20th century, it was mainly the motor manufacturers who entered their own cars in races to prove that theirs were superior to the opposition. But these competitions became an essential part of the vehicle development process.

<<<< **LEFT:** Dan Gurney (Brabham BT7 Climax) in action during his winning race at the 1964 French Grand Prix.

0101010101010
010

The Constructors

As motorsport evolved, the job of designing, building, and refining racing cars was left to specialist engineers; these were often privateers, running small operations funded by wealthy racing enthusiasts. The first set of FIA rules applied from 1946, but the most significant move came in 1950 when the Formula One Championship was launched.

The concept of bringing all elements of racing car construction under a single umbrella—the design, engineering, engine and chassis development, suspension, transmissions, aerodynamics, and even aesthetics—became the norm. And this is what brought the era of the constructor to the fore.

∨ **Below:** Stirling Moss (left, driving a Maserati
∨ 250F) and Juan Manuel Fangio (right, driving
∨ a Mercedes-Benz W196) compete at the
1954 British Grand Prix.

Alfa Romeo dominated the first years of Formula One racing before Alberto Ascari won the next two in a Ferrari. Needless to say, there were winners and losers in the early years of Formula One, as constructors arrived and then withdrew from racing, while a number of tragic accidents and both driver and spectator fatalities highlighted the dangers of the "new" sport.

The key to success in Formula One, as in other forms of motorsport, was squeezing the maximum horsepower from the four-stroke engines that powered the cars. Though some specialist constructors designed and built their own engines, others turned to the motor manufacturers for their help and expertise. For the major industrial companies in Britain, Italy, France, and Germany, it meant a lot to support what were essentially national teams, still racing in national colors.

In the early days of Formula One, there was no such thing as sponsorship. The teams were funded either by themselves or by a parent company and hopefully they would earn enough in winnings to go some way toward covering their costs. Enzo Ferrari was smart enough to realize very early on that it was branding that was crucial to the on-going survival of his racing operation. Every time a Ferrari won on the track, the image of the brand would be enhanced and more cars would be sold both for use on the road or for privateers to take on the track. Outside sponsors started getting involved in Formula One. Many, had an automotive background, and so lubricating oil companies, tire manufacturers, and spark plug manufacturers tended to be the first to get involved.

Even in terms of sponsorship, national pride was an issue so it was no surprise to find an Italian petrol company supporting Ferrari or Alfa Romeo, a British components company sponsoring BRM or Lotus, or a French tire company backing Renault or Matra.

By the 1960s, advertising and sponsorship were so much a natural part of Formula One that companies were almost lining up to put their names on racing cars, but once again it was the great innovator Colin Chapman at Lotus who showed the way forward, painting his car in the colors of the Gold Leaf tobacco brand at Monaco in 1968 in place of the traditional British Racing green. From that moment on, there was no turning back the commercial tide that was encompassing the sport.

160

>>>

Right: Four of the most influential figures in Formula One history in conversation at the 1997 Hungarian Grand Prix: From left to right, Frank Williams, Bernie Ecclestone, Ron Dennis, and Ken Tyrrell.

Formula One racing experienced glory days right through to the 1970s, at which time British teams and British engines started to dominate the championship. Virtually every year the shape and design of cars evolved as constructors vied with each other to produce the purest aerodynamic form. At the same time, structural changes in the sport were being introduced, with race distances being shortened and tracks improved or dropped from the calendar in the name of safety and also to increase spectator appeal.

As the popularity of Formula One around the world continued to grow over the following two decades an increasing number of multinational corporations started taking an interest in the sport. They may have been banks, computer companies or soft drink manufacturers that had no connection with the automotive world but they saw Formula One as a means of spreading their message across the globe. Many millions of pounds, dollars, francs, and marks were injected into the sport, which had two effects. First, it made Formula One an even more competitive business as constructors had more to spend on research and development. But, at the same time, it transformed Formula One into one of the most potentially lucrative businesses in the world.

The teams that managed to attract the millions that the tobacco, drinks and other companies had to spend on publicizing their products and brands, became extremely profitable entities.

In the early days, Formula One was all about speed and victory at any cost. Motorsport was dangerous and occasional accidents—even deaths—were seen as unfortunate, but part and parcel of the sport. But, after the 1994 season when two drivers died and two others were critically injured, the emphasis changed somewhat. The FIA responded rapidly to the crisis and enforced a series of new rules, which were intended to reduce speeds, improve the safety of the cars and impose new and more stringent circuit safety standards.

This has done nothing to diminish Formula One's appeal as the world's leading global motorsport series, with the biggest television audiences, the largest budgets, and arguably the most prestige and glamor too. The top drivers have become world-renowned superstars and new venues have brought places like Bahrain, Shanghai, and Singapore to the world's attention. Yet in many ways it is the constructors who remain the single most important part of the jigsaw. Because in the final analysis, it's they who ensure that throughout the season, the cars are there to line up on the grid, ready for the next round of gladiatorial action.

Above: Filipe Massa (Ferrari F2008) leads during the first lap of the 2008 Brazilian Grand Prix. He went on to win the race.

2005 San Marino Grand Prix: The Renault team celebrates as Fernando Alonso (Renault R25) crosses the line to take victory with Michael Schumacher (Ferrari F2005) close behind.

The 1950s

Formula One began in 1950, two years after the inauguration of a new governing body for motorsport, the FIA. Plans for two championships—constructors and drivers—were unveiled in a bid to provide some structure to the races going on around the world.

The championship united six main European races—Britain, Monaco, Switzerland, Belgium, France, and Italy—with the Indianapolis 500 in the United States.

Left: Jack Brabham (Cooper T51-Climax) leads Tony Brooks (Ferrari Dino 246) and Harry Schell (BRM P25) during the 1959 Dutch Grand Prix.

1950

The first-ever race of the new Formula One world championship took place at the converted airfield of Silverstone, in the heart of Great Britain, and right from the start it was clear that Italian racing red was the order of the day.

Ferrari failed to make it to the opening race at Silverstone, and Alfa filled the first three places on the grid then went on to fill all three places on the podium in Monaco for the second race.

The Indianapolis race was only part of the championship because of its status as one of the world's great races, but none of the European teams turned up and American Johnny Parsons took a victory for Wynn's Kurtis that secured him sixth in the championship. Back in Europe, Alfa men Fangio and Farina traded victories well ahead of the chasing pack and in a dramatic final race at Monza, a gearbox failure for Fangio gave Farina the win and the title by three points.

Below: Alberto Ascari (Ferrari 125, number 40) passes the multi-car accident at the start of the 1950 Monaco Grand Prix.

1951

Ferrari were driving forward, but Alfa still set the early pace in 1951, with Fangio winning in rainy Switzerland.

The first victory for Ferrari finally came at Silverstone when Froilán González capitalized on a mistake by fellow Argentine Fangio. Later, Ascari claimed his first win, because the long straights of the Nürburgring, a new addition to the calendar, suited his Ferrari.

The final race was on the Pedrables street circuit in Spain, which was also destined to be the last race for Alfa before they quit the sport. Thanks to the talent of Fangio and tire problems that beset his title rival Ascari's Ferrari, it was a happy ending for Alfa. The Argentine won, and took the title.

1952

With Alfa gone, Ferrari were now the dominant force in Formula One. The open rules allowed many new teams to join Italians Ferrari and Maserati, with the British Cooper-Bristol in the hands of Mike Hawthorn, and French Gordini machines the best of the rest. But they would never be close enough to challenge the establishment.

Having failed to win at Indianapoils, with victory there going to Troy Ruttman in his Kurtis-Kraft, Ascari returned for round three, in Belgium, and dominated the rest of the season with an amazing run of six consecutive race victories, with the fastest lap in every one.

He mastered the wet in Spa then led a Ferrari 1-2-3 in France and a 1-2 in Britain. Victories in Holland and Italy finished off a remarkable run of dominance and, with only the best four results counting, Ascari notched up a perfect score.

1953

Ascari was the man to beat again in 1953, but the return of Juan Manuel Fangio with Maserati saw the Italian teams' rivalry strengthen as the season progressed.

The championship expanded into new territory, going to South America for the first time with a race in Argentina.

Ascari won again in Britain and probably would have taken victory in Germany had his wheel not fallen off, handing victory to Farina. However, Ascari secured the title in style at the last but one race in Switzerland, when an unscheduled stop forced him to fight through the field, past Farina and Hawthorn, to claim victory.

In the final race of the year, in Italy, a spectacular slipstreaming battle saw Ascari assume the lead, but he made a mistake on the last lap and spun, taking out team-mate Farina in the process, and letting Fangio through to take Maserati's debut win.

<<<<

Left: Mike Hawthorn (Cooper T20-Bristol) leads Giuseppe Farina (Ferrari 500) during the 1952 Dutch Grand Prix.

1954

1954 saw Mercedes-Benz make its Formula One debut. The uniquely attractive 'streamliner' machines drew Fangio away from Maserati while Ascari was tempted by the promise of new arrival Lancia.

The Mercedes struggled at Silverstone, leaving Gonzalez to claim victory for Ferrari. Sadly, Formula One was again hit by tragedy at the following race in Germany, when Argentine Maserati driver Onofre Marimón became the first driver to die at a Formula One event.

Fangio fought back the tears for his countryman and raced to victory, then went from strength to strength, winning in Switzerland and Italy.

1955

The 1955 season is remembered for tragedy rather than triumph. World motorsport was rocked by the deaths of more than 80 people at Le Mans as well as the loss of former champion Ascari, who crashed testing a sports car, mid season.

But the racing went on with Fangio firm favorite for Mercedes.

Fangio and Moss took a 1-2 for Mercedes in Belgium and though the next weekend saw the tragedy at Le Mans, Formula One raced on, with Mercedes dominating to claim a 1-2 in Holland, a 1-2-3-4 in Britain—with Moss claiming his maiden win on home soil—and closing the season off with a 1-2 on the circuit of Monza, handing Fangio his second consecutive title.

1956

This year brought a huge shock to the sport as Mercedes pulled out at the end of their second title-winning season, leaving Fangio fleeing to former enemy Ferrari, who decided to use the Lancia chassis. Meanwhile, Moss made a move to Maserati and Hawthorn had another stab at fighting the British corner by moving across to BRM.

The final round, at Monza, saw a unique finish to the championship when Fangio retired with a broken steering arm. Behra also dropped out and Collins, who could have won the title, pulled into the pits and gave the car over to Fangio to hand the Argentine another world championship crown.

Below Jose Froilán Gonzaléz (Ferrari 625) leads Juan Manuel Fangio (Mercedes-Benz W196) and Stirling Moss (Maserati 250F) at the start of the 1954 German Grand Prix.

1957

Argentine Fangio made it four wins in a row at home with victory in Buenos Aires as Maserati finished 1-2-3-4 and Ferrari faltered with mechanical problems. Across the Atlantic, the Indy 500 was won by Sam Hanks in his Epperly machine while, back in Europe, the circus moved on to France for another dominant Fangio victory, though the two Vanwall drivers, Moss and Tony Brooks, were notably missing from the grid.

Fangio put on his best ever display in Germany, and secured his fifth and final title when he was second to Moss in the penultimate race at Pescara. The pair then finished the season in style, with Moss taking the win after a spectacular battle at Monza.

Below: The field taking the curve after the Raidillon de l'eau Rouge in the 1956 Belgian Grand Prix.

1958

It was the end of an era when Fangio and Maserati retired from Formula One in 1958.

In the longest Formula One season so far, Vanwall seemed to be Ferrari's only rivals, but it was a rear-engined Cooper-Climax 43 (as opposed to the then-standard front-engined design) that claimed the first victory with Moss at the wheel.

It was not going to plan for Ferrari and, though they won in France, with Hawthorn taking his only victory of the year, tragedy struck as Musso was killed. Briton Collins won for Ferrari at Silverstone but, just two weeks later, he was also killed, becoming the second Ferrari driver to lose his life in a month.

1959

The end of the decade marked a true phase shift in Formula One as the rear-engined Cooper-Climax, with a new 2.5-liter engine, came to the fore.

Vanwall had quit and Brooks had joined Ferrari, along with Behra and American Phil Hill, but their front-engined machine failed to perform and a new grid order was created.

Below: The 1958 Monaco Grand Prix: Maurice Trintignant receives the winning trophy from HRH Prince Rainier and Princess Grace.

The 1960s

This 10-year period saw Formula One go through what could be seen as the most significant technical developments in its history. British teams led the way and the sport began to build its reputation as the place for innovation at the pinnacle of motorsport.

The arrival of sponsorship put an end to teams racing in national colors and, as the sport headed into the 1970s, the 13-race calendar could now claim to be fully global, with a core in Europe, but races also run in South Africa, Canada, the United States, and Mexico.

<<< **Left:** The cars line up on the grid before the start of the 1966 British Grand Prix.

1960

The success of Jack Brabham and his Cooper at the end of the 1950s left nobody in any doubt that the front-engined car had had its day. Nevertheless, Ferrari persisted and got nowhere. Instead, Cooper and the new rear-engined Lotus dominated, with Brabham and Bruce McLaren taking on Moss and Innes Ireland.

The European field now included Belgium, but it was one of the worst races in history. Moss had a leg-breaking crash; then, as Brabham raced from pole to victory, Chris Bristow and Alan Stacey were killed, the latter after his helmet was hit by a bird.

Brabham claimed further victories in France, Britain, and Portugal, where he won the title with two races to go. With the championship over, the British teams boycotted the Italian race due to safety concerns, so Phil Hill won for Ferrari while Moss returned to finish off the season with victory at the final round in the United States.

Below: Jack Brabham (Cooper T53 Climax) on his way to victory in the 1960 Monaco Grand Prix.

1961

Ferrari had a very successful season creating their "sharknose" car specifically for the new 1.5-liter formula.

The season opened in Monaco and Moss, in a privateer Lotus, overcame his inferior machinery to take the win. But Ferrari came back strong with a 1-2 for Wolfgang von Trips and Phil Hill in Holland, then finished 1-2-3-4 as Hill took victory in Belgium.

Ferrari were back on top in Britain with von Trips leading a 1-2-3 finish, but Moss fought back in Germany to win for Climax.

Then came Monza, and tragedy. Von Trips took pole but collided with Clark's Lotus at the Parabolica and his Ferrari rolled. He was thrown from the car and was killed along with 15 spectators.

>>>>

Left: Spectators look at the Ferrari of German driver Wolfgang von Trips after it crashed into the crowd killing 15 people during the Italian Formula One Grand Prix, on September 10, 1961 in Monza.

1962

A tough and emotional end to 1961 saw Ferrari in turmoil and Moss, perhaps the greatest driver never to win a title, deciding to quit after a pre-season crash.

Englishman Graham Hill took first blood in the battle when he won the season opener for BRM. McLaren drove his Cooper to victory in Monaco, but Clark claimed his first-ever win—for Lotus— in Belgium, after a five-car slipstreaming battle.

Gurney gave Porsche a historic first win in France, inheriting the victory after three leaders dropped out to make the German team the year's fourth different winner. South Africa held the final race and Clark looked strong for victory, having led from pole, until his engine failed and handed Hill, and BRM, the championship title. Having won the title the previous year, Ferrari failed to even win a race and scored just 18 points.

Right: Jack Brabham (left, no. 16) and Carel Godin de Beaufort (right, no. 18) take shelter from the rain before the start of the 1962 German Grand Prix. >>>>

1963

There was no doubting Clark's driving talent and, once Lotus found the reliability, it was destined to be a title-winning partnership. The season did not start well for Clark, with gearbox problems halting his charge from pole at Monaco, handing victory to Hill and a BRM 1-2. His fortunes changed and he claimed his first victory of the year, then followed it with comfortable wins in Holland, France, and Britain.

The Italian team took a new car to Monza for their home race, but its engine failed and Clark won to claim his first championship title, three races before the season finished. Hill's BRM finally found some reliability for him to win in the United States, but Clark rounded out the season with victories in Mexico and South Africa.

1964

Clark and Hill carried on where they left off the season before, but reliability problems for Lotus and BRM coupled with a late resurgence from Ferrari—who had looked out of the fight early in the season—saw the title go right down to the wire.

Hill started the season with victory in Monaco as Clark suffered an engine failure. But the Scot was soon back, winning in Holland, then inheriting victory in Belgium after Gurney, Hill, and McLaren had all dropped out of the lead with fuel problems in the final two laps.

Victories for Surtees in Germany and Italy sandwiched a win for team-mate, Bandini, in Austria, a race where Hill, Surtees, and Clark all failed to finish. Clark looked set for the title. Then his engine failed one lap from the end and, with Bandini moving over to concede second, Surtees took the title.

1965

Clark was unstoppable from the start, with a Lotus car that seemed unbreakable and a Climax engine that put the power back into the hands of the British teams. Ferrari failed to perform, while Honda arrived, luring Richie Ginther from BRM, who, in turn hired Jackie Stewart.

Clark retired from the remaining three races with engine failure, which allowed Stewart to score his maiden win in Monza, Hill to win a third race for BRM in the United States, and Ginther to claim the first-ever race victory for both Honda and tire supplier Goodyear in Mexico.

>>>>

Right: Jack Brabham (Brabham BT19 Repco)—who won the race—leads Denny Hulme (Brabham BT20 Repco), Jim Clark (Lotus 33 Climax), and Graham Hill (BRM P261) during the 1966 Dutch Grand Prix.

1966

Stewart won the opening race in Monaco for BRM, but the second race was at a rain-hit Spa circuit in Belgium and the Scot had a terrible crash that sidelined him for two months. Surtees won in what would be his last race for Ferrari before his switch to Cooper.

All the title contenders, including Brabham, retired from the race at Monza, handing Surtees his third world title as rookie Ludovico Scarfiotti won for Ferrari.

1967

The arrival of the new Lotus 49 coupled with a revolutionary Cosworth DFV engine tempted Hill to join rival Clark in what many saw as the dream team for 1967.

Hulme took early victories for Brabham and the championship moved on to Holland, where the Lotus 49 made its debut and Clark drove to victory.

Reliability problems marred the Lotus season. Clark ran out of fuel while leading at Monza, handing victory to Surtees and Honda, then the Lotus finally found some reliability, which allowed Clark to lead a 1-2. But it was too little, too late, and Hulme claimed the crown.

Below: Jackie Stewart (BRM P83) before the start of the 1967 British Grand Prix.

1968

Hill, now racing in a newly sponsored red, white, and gold Lotus fitted with aerodynamic wings, scored victories in Spain and Monaco. Racing continued, and after Jo Siffert won in Britain in a private Lotus, Stewart took victory at Germany's Nürburgring and Hulme won in Monza and Canada, moving him level with Hill in the championship.

Victory in the United States for Stewart set up a three-way season-ending title battle in Mexico. Hulme crashed out early, but Stewart and Hill vied for the lead until the Scot suffered handling problems and dropped down the order, leaving Hill to win the title.

1969

Stewart dominated the season opener in South Africa, then won again in Spain after Ferrari suffered engine problems and the two Lotus cars crashed heavily after failures to their high-mounted wings, which were subsequently banned from the sport.

Hill claimed his fifth win in Monaco, but it was just a minor break in Stewart's rhythm, and the Scot raced to further victories in Holland, France, and Britain. Ickx won in Canada after knocking Stewart out of the race and Rindt won in the United States, in a race marred by a major accident that saw Hill break both legs. He missed the season finale in Mexico, which was won by Hulme for McLaren.

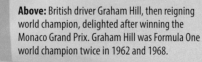

Above: British driver Graham Hill, then reigning world champion, delighted after winning the Monaco Grand Prix. Graham Hill was Formula One world champion twice in 1962 and 1968.

Graham Hill leads Jo Siffert (both Lotus 49B Ford) and Jackie Stewart (Matra MS10 Ford) during the 1968 Mexican Grand Prix. They finished in first, sixth, and seventh positions respectively.

The
1970s

Danger was still a real concern for motorsport at the start of the 1970s, but until the incumbent Formula One champion Jackie Stewart retired and began his campaign for improvements, death was almost considered an unfortunate but unavoidable part of the sport.

Developments focused on speed and the advancement of aerodynamics was dramatic, changing the look of the cars significantly. The calendar continued to expand, increasing to between 16 and 17 races, with Brazil and Japan arriving to make the series increasingly more global.

<<<< McLaren Ford driver James Hunt is involved in a pile up during the Formula One British Grand Prix at Brands Hatch in Kent, England, 1976.

1970

Stewart put the new March on pole at the season opener in South Africa, but dropped to third as Brabham stormed through to claim victory in the race itself.

Brabham returned to form in Monaco only to see his heroic defence of first place end when he crashed and allowed Rindt through to take the win. Soon after, Formula One lost one of its biggest names when Bruce McLaren was killed testing a Can-Am car at Goodwood.

A tragic practice crash claimed the life of 28-year-old Rindt ahead of the next race, in Italy, and Clay Regazzoni took a hollow victory for Ferrari. As the season progressed Ickx won in Canada, but a retirement in the last but one race in the United States ended his title chances and Rindt was named the sport's first posthumous champion.

∨ **Below:** Jackie Stewart (March
∨ 701 Ford) on his way to victory in
∨ the 1970 Spanish Grand Prix.

1971

Tyrrell decided to go it alone after a promising test for his own car at the end of the previous season and it proved to be a wise decision, as Stewart dominated and the rest of the field failed to produce a consistently strong contender.

Stewart won in France, Britain, and Germany, twice leading team-mate François Cevert home in a 1-2 for Tyrrell. BRM managed to stop his run of success when Jo Siffert won in Austria, but when Ickx retired from the race, the championship went to Stewart.

Peter Gethin snatched victory from Peterson by 0.01s in Italy as the top five cars crossed the line within 0.61s of each other. Stewart retired with engine failure in Monza, but won in Canada while his team-mate Cevery claimed his first win at the season finale in the United States.

1972

Bernie Ecclestone became team manager of Brabham and when Formula One returned to Argentina for race one, his home driver Carlos Reutermann took pole, though reigning champion Stewart raced past to win for Tyrrell.

However, Fittipaldi would soon stamp his authority with victory in four of the following six races. The Brazilian won in Belgium, with Stewart sidelined by a stomach ulcer, the consistent Fittipaldi extended his title lead over Stewart by winning in Austria then sealed the crown with victory in Monza.

1973

Lotus hoped to dominate when Peterson joined Fittipaldi in the 'dream team' and, though McLaren, Brabham, and March were all in the mix, it was the resurgent Stewart, in his Tyrrell, who led the fight to stop them.

Lotus returned to form in Austria, where Peterson waved Fittipaldi through for the sake of the title only for the Brazilian to retire. The pair finished 1-2 in Italy, but the title battle was over. The season wasn't, and after Revson won in the Canadian race Cevert was killed in practice in the United States. Peterson won, but the death of Stewart's team-mate vindicated the Scot's decision to quit.

Above: François Cevert (Tyrrell 006 Ford Cosworth) in action during the 1973 British Grand Prix.

1974

Fittipaldi moved from Lotus to McLaren when the team lured the major Marlboro sponsorship funding away from BRM. There was change at Ferrari, too, with a brand new car and the arrival of Regazzoni and Niki Lauda.

Peterson and Scheckter took second victories in France and Britain respectively, before Regazzoni finally won for Ferrari in Germany.

Reutermann won in Austria and Peterson in Italy but, after finishing first and second in Canada, Regazzoni and Fittipaldi fought for the title in the United States finale. They were level on points, but a disappointing finish saw Regazzoni drop down the field with handling problems, leaving Fittipaldi finishing fourth to claim the title.

Below: Emerson Fittipaldi crosses the finish line ahead of Niki Lauda, to take the win at the 1974 Belgian Grand Prix.

1975

After several years of British success, Ferrari introduced the new longitudinal gearboxed 312T and was ready to return to form. Lauda grew into a fine team leader, but a season to savour for the Italian giants was hit by more fatalities, making it a sad year for everyone involved in Formula One.

1976

Ferrari's champion Lauda faced a tough challenge from James Hunt in 1976 after the Briton replaced Fittipaldi at McLaren. In a nail-biting battle, Lauda suffered a serious accident but came back to take the championship right down to the wire.

Hunt started strongly, putting his McLaren on pole in Argentina and South Africa, but both times he lost out to Lauda in the race, then Regazzoni made it three for Ferrari with victory at a new Long Beach street race in the United States.

Lauda was well on course for the title when he crashed in Germany and suffered severe burns. Hunt moved to within three points of the lead, winning in Canada and the United States then, when Lauda pulled out of the last race in Japan on safety grounds after a torrential downpour, Hunt raced on and claimed the third place he needed to take the title.

>>>>

Right: James Hunt (McLaren M23 Ford) leads John Watson (Penske PC4 Ford) on his way to victory in the 1976 Dutch Grand Prix.

1977

1978

Ferrari and Lauda put together a consistent campaign in a season that saw eight different winners from the 17 races. However, the year was again tainted by driver and spectator deaths.

A horrific accident in South Africa killed Tom Pryce and a track marshal. Then, sadly, Pace died in a plane crash before the next race.

Lauda won for Ferrari in Germany and Holland and took second places in Austria, where Alan Jones gave Shadow a first win, and Italy, where Andretti finished first for Lotus. Lauda had been third or better in all but one of the races he had finished and he secured the title with fourth place in the United States, a race won by Hunt.

Ferrari introduced the new 312T3 in a bid to retain their superiority, but Lotus took another step forward with the revolutionary 79 and soon began to dominate the season. Their success, however, was soured by the tragic death of Ronnie Peterson.

A double Lotus retirement let Reutermann win for Ferrari in Britain, but Lotus then won in Germany, Austria, and Holland; the latter being their fourth 1-2 of the year as Peterson was forced to play second fiddle to Andretti. Only Peterson could beat Andretti to the title, but a fiery start-line crash in Italy saw him suffer terrible burns and, despite being quickly dragged from the wreckage by Hunt, Regazzoni, and Depallier, he died the following day.

Andretti was crowned Champion, but it was the Ferraris of Reutermann and Villeneuve that went on to win the last two races, in the US and Canada.

1979

The season started with victories for Laffitte's Ligier in Argentina and Brazil, but Ferrari introduced their new car for race three and Villeneuve led 1-2 finishes in South Africa and the United States. Ligier won again with Depallier in Spain, but Scheckter got his first Ferrari win in Belgium and followed it up with victory in Monaco.

Formula One history was made at Dijon in France, when the usually unreliable Renault made it across the finish line to claim the first-ever turbo-powered victory, with Jean-Pierre Jabouille leading home Arnoux after a dramatic wheel-to-wheel battle.

The new Williams FW07 had been competitive ever since its Belgian debut and in Britain, Jones put it on pole before Regazzoni secured the team their first-ever victory.

Scheckter took what would be Ferrari's last title for 21 years when he won in Italy, finishing just 0.46s ahead of Villeneuve in a Ferrari 1-2 as team tactics came into play.

<<<<
Left: Niki Lauda (Ferrari 312T2) battles with Mario Andretti (Lotus 78 Ford) on his way to winning the 1977 Dutch Grand Prix.

James Hunt (McLaren M23 Ford) locks up and takes off over the front wheel of John Watson's Brabham BT45B Alfa Romeo, in the chain reaction of collisions at Cooks Corner on the first lap of the 1977 United States Grand Prix.

The
1980s

The start of the decade was overshadowed by political rows as the manufacturer teams and the privateers vied for supremacy. The manufacturers, led by Ferrari, Renault and Alfa Romeo, were pushing for a limitation in the use of ground-effect aerodynamics, to help make the most of their turbo engines; while the smaller teams wanted no restrictions because they could not afford the cost of developing the new high-power engines.

Tragic accidents in the early 80s cut short the career of Didier Pironi and cost Gilles Villeneuve his life, leaving Brazilians Ayrton Senna and Nelson Piquet, Frenchman Alain Prost, and Briton Nigel Mansell as the men to watch.

<<<< **Left:** Gerhard Berger (Ferrari F187/88C) holds off Alain Prost (McLaren MP4/4 Honda) as they race through Casino Square during the 1988 Monaco Grand Prix. Prost went on to win the race.

1980

Williams built on the form they showed at the end of the 1970s while champions Ferrari lost their way and even failed to qualify for one race. Alfa Romeo returned and Brabham stepped up to the front. Safety continued to be an issue with several top drivers killed, paralysed, or lucky to escape.

Regazzoni's career was ended at the next race in the United States when he crashed and was left paralysed. Piquet scored his first victory in that race, for Brabham, then Pironi took his maiden win, for Ligier, in Belgium. Williams then began a run of victories when Reutermann took the spoils in Monaco and though Jones' victory in Spain was declared void after the turbo teams refused to take part, he went on to win in France and Britain.

Depallier died in a testing crash before the German race, which was won by Laffite, then Jean-Pierre Jabouille won for Renault in Austria.

The championship was decided in the next three races, with Piquet taking the lead by a point after wins in Holland and Italy and setting up a dramatic race in Canada. Jones and Piquet collided on the first lap, causing a race stoppage, but Piquet retired from the restart and Jones won the race then finished off in style with victory in the United States.

Below: Alan Jones (Williams FW07B-Ford Cosworth) in the 1980 British Grand Prix.

1981

Williams and Brabham led the way in 1981, but off-track disputes made more headlines than the racing as FISA and FOCA went to war. The season got off to a false start when the FISA teams pulled out of the first round in South Africa, and the championship started properly in the United States instead.

Villeneuve took surprise wins for Ferrari in Monaco and Spain then, in France, Renault driver Prost took his first victory in a rain-affected race of two halves. Briton John Watson was victorious on home soil for McLaren, Piquet won in Germany, and Laffitte became the seventh different winner in 11 races with victory in Austria.

The final race went to Jones but in the title race Piquet picked up the points he needed to take the crown.

Above: Nelson Piquet (Brabham BT49C-Ford Cosworth) on his way to fifth position, and the World Championship win, in the 1981 Las Vegas Grand Prix.

1985

After narrowly losing out on the last two occasions, Prost was hoping for third time lucky in 1985, but he faced strong competition as Rosberg was joined by Mansell at Williams, Senna took the Briton's place at Lotus, and Alboreto led the Ferrari charge after Arnoux quit the team one race into the season. Prost's consistency, with podiums in all his 11 scoring races, won him the title.

1987

The field was split between turbo and non-turbo cars in preparation for a turbo ban in 1989, but Williams kept their high powered Honda engine and dominated. Increasingly bitter rivalry developed between team-mates Mansell and Piquet and a dramatic battle for the title went down to the penultimate race of the season.

Mansell won in Spain, with Piquet fourth, and led a Williams 1-2 in Mexico, but injured his back in a practice crash in Japan. His title bid was over. Piquet failed to finish again as Berger won in Japan and Australia, but he had already done enough.

1986

It was a classic year-long battle for the title in 1986. Rosberg replaced the retired Lauda at McLaren, but he was outshone by Prost with the Williams-Hondas of Mansell and Piquet, who arrived from Brabham, and Senna's Lotus; making it a four way fight that went to the wire at a spectacular season-ending race.

At the final race in Australia, Mansell had a seven-point lead, but it was still possible that either Piquet or Prost could steal the title. Mansell took pole, but dropped out of the race when his tire blew. Williams pulled Piquet in for a safety check and Prost—who had suffered a puncture himself—stormed through to take the title by two points.

>>>>

Right: Alain Prost (McLaren MP4/2B TAG Porsche) on his way to winning the 1985 Austrian Grand Prix.

1988

McLaren took Honda from Williams for 1988 and Senna joined Prost in a new super team that completely crushed the opposition, winning 15 of the 16 races as Williams descended from dominant champions to mid-grid mediocrity.

Heavy rain at Silverstone saw Prost stop on safety grounds as Senna won ahead of Mansell in a shock second. Senna then took a hat-trick of wins in Germany, Hungary, and Belgium before his domination was stopped by a back marker in Italy and Ferrari scored a poignant 1-2 just weeks after Enzo Ferrari passed away.

Prost then looked set for victory in Japan when Senna dropped to 14th at the start but Senna raced back and overtook Prost to win. Senna—with 90 points and eight wins— had done enough to win his first title.

Below: Alain Prost (McLaren MP4/4 Honda) celebrates his victory in the 1988 Australian Grand Prix at Adelaide.

1989

A move to the new 3.5-liter non-turbo formula failed to stop another season of McLaren domination, but the rivalry between Senna and Prost boiled over as they tried to out-do each other in every way possible.

Mansell joined Ferrari with instant success, but the Italian team was not strong enough to mount a title challenge. Senna went on to dominant wins in Monaco and Mexico, but it was not to last and he suffered four retirements as Prost won in the United States, Boutsen broke McLaren's domination with a Williams 1-2 in Canada, and Prost won again in France and Britain.

Berger won in Portugal after Mansell took out Senna, leaving Prost with a 24-point lead. Senna would not give up and won in Spain then battled Prost for victory in Japan. The pair collided, putting Prost out, but Senna came back to win only to be disqualified, handing victory to Nannini's Benetton and the title to Prost.

Below: Ayrton Senna leads into the first corner followed by team-mate Alain Prost (both McLaren MP4/5 Honda) during the 1989 Belgian Grand Prix. Senna finished in first place and Prost in second.

The 1990s

The decade began with the separation of one of the sport's strongest ever driver line-ups as Prost left Senna at McLaren to join Ferrari. The pair continued to fight for supremacy both on and off the track, battling for wins while vying with each other to get the best seat at Williams, as their technologically advanced cars moved to the front. But everything was to change at Imola in 1994 in one of the most shocking weekends Formula One has ever seen.

Improvements in safety had made the sport complacent and the deaths of Senna and Roland Ratzenberger, who both perished at San Marino, instigated fundamental change.

Left: Benetton mechanic Paul Seaby is engulfed in flames during a disastrous Jos Verstappen pit stop at the 1994 German Grand Prix. Amazingly, Seaby survived the accident with only minor burns.

1990

After his controversial clash with Prost in Japan in 1989, Senna was facing a ban. He received a late reprieve and lined up with Berger at McLaren, with Prost now at Ferrari, but the end of the season proved that a leopard cannot change its spots. Senna started with victory in Phoenix, but Prost then took his first Ferrari win in Brazil, on Senna's home soil.

Prost won in Spain, and then came Japan. The pair lined up on row one, but when Senna started slowly he refused to concede the corner. They collided and Senna won the title. Piquet won the race for Benetton, as he did in Australia, but the Japan collision tarnished Senna's reputation.

1991

Reigning champion Senna was concerned by the pace of his new McLaren, but a great opening run put him in the driving seat early on. Senna took pole and victories in the first four races, but Piquet and Benetton broke the stranglehold in Canada.

Spa saw the debut of Michael Schumacher who, driving for the new Jordan team, qualified seventh but retired on lap one. Mansell hit back in Italy, where Schumacher scored his first points in fifth after moving to Benetton.
Senna won the title and handed victory in Japan to team-mate Berger before winning a shortened race in terrible conditions in Australia.

Above: Jean Alesi (Tyrrell 018 Ford) laps backmarker Michele Alboreto (Arrows A11B Ford) with Ayrton Senna (Mclaren MP4/5B Honda) hot on his heels behind at the 1990 United States Grand Prix.

1992

There was no stopping the dominant Williams' cars this time, with some of the most technologically advanced equipment seen in the sport helping Mansell and Patrese to win after win. And while Senna battled hard for McLaren, it was Michael Schumacher who came closest to the leading duo.

Schumacher scored a maiden victory in Belgium by picking the right strategy in variable wet-dry conditions then Senna won in Italy. Mansell won in Portugal to break the record number of wins in a season, then Patrese and Berger won in Japan and Australia to bring the season to an end.

Below: 1992 San Marino Grand Prix: Nigel Mansell (Williams FW14B Renault) on his way to setting a new record of winning five consecutive Grand Prix from the start of the season.

1993

Williams continued to dominate, with Prost and Damon Hill teaming up for the 1993 season. Senna took the fight to his old rival in the Ford-powered McLaren after deciding to drive on a race-by-race basis.

Prost was back in the groove in San Marino, winning in the dry, and he won again in Spain before Senna took his sixth Monaco win. Schumacher won in Portugal, but Prost finished close behind in second and, on winning the title, announced his retirement.

Below: Michael Schumacher (Benetton B194 Ford) crashes at a chicane during a practice session for the 1994 Australian Grand Prix.

1994

Senna joined Williams to create one of the most hotly anticipated car-driver combinations, but the car suffered from a ban on driver aids. Three races in, Senna was killed and Schumacher, despite running a Bennetton-Ford car inferior to the Williams-Renault, was left to take over the mantle of a legend.

The sport was shocked when Roland Ratzenberger died after crashing in Saturday practice at San Marino, then Senna crashed during the race. Schumacher continued on to victory, but then news came through that Senna had died. Berger took Ferrari's first win in 58 races in Germany after a dramatic 11-car pile-up. Schumacher took victory in Hungary but Hill then won three in a row, with Schumacher disqualified in Spa and suspended in Italy and Portugal. Schumacher won the European Grand Prix, but Hill won in Japan. At the final race in Australia, with one point between them, the pair collided and Schumacher won his first title as the returning Mansell took his final race victory.

1995

The FIA introduced safety improvements to cars after the tragic 1994 season, including reducing engine capacity to 3-liters and raising ride height with a stepped bottom, but the Williams-Renault cars remained the class of the field.

Hill started strongly and, though his suspension failure handed Schumacher victory in Brazil, he dominated Argentina and San Marino. Schumacher crashed at Imola, but was back in Spain for a Benetton 1-2 after hydraulics problems hit both Williams cars. That race saw Mansell retire for good after a disastrous time with McLaren. Schumacher sealed the title with a Pacific Grand Prix win and celebrated with victory in Japan before Hill took a consolation prize in Australia, winning by two laps as just eight drivers finished.

Below: Ayrton Senna (Williams FW16 Renault) at the 1994 San Marino Grand Prix, before he was tragically killed in an accident on the start of lap seven.

1996

Schumacher took on a new challenge at Ferrari in 1996 as he and Eddie Irvine replaced Benetton-bound Berger and Alesi. It took time for the German to move the struggling team to the front and, with a lack of opposition for the dominant Williams cars, Damon Hill only had his new team-mate Jacques Villeneuve to beat.

Schumacher mastered drying conditions to win a three-way battle in Belgium, then won in Italy after Hill crashed out. Villeneuve led a Williams 1-2 in Portugal to take the title to the wire but Hill, who needed just one point, won in Japan to become the first second-generation World Champion.

Below: Damon Hill (Williams FW18 Renault) on his way to victory in the 1996 Canadian Grand Prix.

 1997

Champion Hill was shown the door as Williams welcomed Heinz-Harald Frentzen and the Briton decided to take a gamble on Arrows-Yamaha. Villeneuve took control, but Ferrari were becoming a force and Schumacher took a 'do or die' approach as the title went to the wire.

Schumacher dominated Monaco in the wet as the Williams and McLaren cars crashed and Stewart finished second in their fifth race. Panis challenged Villeneuve for victory in Spain, but lost and then suffered a leg-breaking crash in Canada as Schumacher raced to victory.

Wins in Austria and Luxembourg put Villeneuve closer, but disqualification for passing under waved yellows in Japan saw Schumacher move ahead with victory. Following a controversial incident during lap 48 of the European Grand Prix, where Schumacher turned into Villeneuve, causing a collision, Schumacher was disqualified from the 1997 World Championship and Villeneuve continued and claimed the title.

>>>>

Right: Mika Häkkinen crosses the line ahead of team-mate David Coulthard (both McLaren MP4/12 Mercedes) to win the 1997 European Grand Prix.

1998

The season saw cars narrowed and grooved tires introduced to reduce increasing speeds.

Schumacher began a hat-trick of wins when both McLarens failed in Canada. He won fair and square in France, then took a confused victory in Britain, ahead of Häkkinen, after the FIA failed to add a time penalty for pit-line speeding.
Häkkinen fought back to lead McLaren 1-2s in Austria and Germany, but Schumacher took a strategic victory in Hungary.

Schumacher led a 1-2 for Ferrari in Italy after champion Villeneuve, still without a win, spun out of the lead. Häkkinen beat Schumacher in Luxembourg. By now his lead was four points with only Japan to go. Schumacher had to fight from the back after stalling on the grid, but his hopes went when a tire failed, leaving Häkkinen to win the race and the title.

>>>>

Right: Mika Häkkinen celebrates winning the 1998 Australian Grand Prix

1999

The decade closed as it began, with a clear battle between McLaren and Ferrari, but mid-season disaster for Schumacher left Irvine taking Ferrari's charge to the wire. Williams faltered and Jordan stepped up, with Frentzen joining Hill to become real contenders, while Villeneuve's promising new BAR team failed to deliver.

Schumacher's title challenge hit the skids in Britain when a leg-breaking crash put him out for six races. Coulthard won after pit mistakes by Häkkinen and Irvine, and when the McLaren pair collided at the start in Austria, Irvine took the win.

Frentzen won for Jordan in Italy, then Herbert took Stewart's first victory in a wet European Grand Prix. Schumacher returned for the new Malaysia race and fended off Häkkinen as Irvine led a Ferrari 1-2, but the Ulsterman failed at the final hurdle in Japan. Häkkinen took the title with a win as Irvine managed only third. Nevertheless, Ferrari was the constructors' champion as Formula One headed toward a new era.

Below: 1999 Malaysian Grand Prix: Eddie Irvine (Ferrari F399) closely followed by Mika Hakkinen (McLaren MP4/14 Mercedes). They finished in first and third positions respectively.

Michael Schumacher (Benetton B195 Renault) takes the checkered flag to win the 1995 French Grand Prix at Magny-Cours.

The 2000s

Michael Schumacher re-wrote the record books at Ferrari in his ruthless pursuit of a record seven World Driver's Championships. McLaren and Williams took the early fight to Ferrari, but new rivals emerged as the motor manufacturers moved in. Toyota created an all-new team, while Jaguar took over from Stewart, Renault from Benetton, Honda from BAR, and BMW from Sauber, while Mercedes united strongly with McLaren.

The calendar continued to grow, up to 19 races at one stage but, as it consolidated, some traditional races lost their place and new locations such as China, Bahrain, Turkey, and Singapore arrived.

Left: Michael Schumacher (Ferrari F2004) on his way to winning the 2004 Hungarian Grand Prix. This was the seventh consecutive race that Schumacher won in 2004.

2000

Schumacher led a Ferrari 1-2 in Australia as both McLarens retired, then won easily in Brazil and again in San Marino.

Schumacher won an emotional race in Italy, then took a record 42nd win as the sport returned to Indianapolis. He beat Häkkinen in Japan to seal the drivers' title, Ferrari's first since 1979, then celebrated with victory as the season ended in Malaysia.

2001

Schumacher was dominant in his title defence during a year in which traction control returned and Fernando Alonso and Kimi Räikkönen made significant debuts.

Häkkinen and McLaren returned to form in Britain and Ralf Schumacher won in Germany but, when Michael won the next race in Hungary, the title was his. He won again in Belgium and the season wrapped up with Montoya finally taking his maiden win in Italy.

2002

Ferrari were in a class of their own, both on pace and reliability. Schumacher finished every race, winning 11, with podiums in the rest.

However, team orders caused controversy, first in Austria where Barrichello was forced to move over for Schumacher.

Ferrari shamed themselves again in the United States, when Schumacher slowed to cross the line alongside Barrichello and the Brazilian accidentally overtook him to win.

2003

New rules including one-lap qualifying and a points structure were introduced to make the sport more entertaining.

Coulthard won for McLaren in Australia, with Ferrari off the podium for the first time since 1999. Schumacher returned to form in San Marino, Spain, Austria, and Canada, separated by Montoya's Monaco victory.

The top three contenders were separated by two points with three races to run, but then Schumacher led a Ferrari resurgence, winning in Italy and the United States, and got the point he needed to take the title in a rain-hit finale in Japan.

Below: David Coulthard leads Mika Häkkinen (both McLaren MP4/15 Mercedes) at the 2000 British Grand Prix. They finished in first and second positions respectively.

2004

The drama of 2003 was replaced by dull domination as Ferrari and Bridgestone made Schumacher awe-inspiringly unstoppable, winning 12 of the first 13 races with Barrichello backing him up again.

Räikkönen's win in Belgium for the out-of-form McLaren ended Schumacher's run, but second was enough to seal a record seventh driver's crown.

160

2005

Ferrari faced a backlash after a dominant 2004 and, in a season with the most races ever, Renault enjoyed a consistent campaign and McLaren-Mercedes produced a fast but fragile car to give Räikkönen and new team-mate Montoya joy and despair in equal measure.

Schumacher's dismal season was hardly brightened by victory in a farcical United States Grand Prix after all Michelin runners pulled out on safety grounds. Räikkönen clawed 10 points back by winning in Hungary, but while McLaren then dominated with wins for Räikkönen in Turkey, Belgium, and Japan and Montoya in Italy, Alonso was crowned champion when he finished third behind a McLaren 1-2 in Brazil.

Below: Fernando Alonso (Renault R24) forces an error from Felipe Massa (Sauber Petronas C23) during the 2004 Bahrain Grand Prix.

2006

Bidding for an eighth title, Schumacher matched Alonso at the head of the field, the pair filling the top two places in eight of 18 races as the old champion took the new one right down to the wire. The season saw the arrival of BMW, Honda, Toro Rosso, and Super Aguri while Jordan became Midland then Spyker.

Renault won the first three races, but Schumacher won in San Marino and Europe before Alonso embarked on a run of four. Ferrari and Schumacher fought back in the United States, then won again in France and Germany.

Schumacher closed the title gap with wins in Italy, where Alonso retired, and China, but retired in Japan and his long shot at the title went when Alonso won it with second in Brazil as Renault took the constructors' crown.

Above: Fernando Alonso (Renault R26) leads Michael Schumacher (Ferrari 248) and Giancarlo Fisichella (Renault R26) on his way to victory in the 2006 Brazilian Grand Prix.

2007

Alonso left Renault to create a turbulent partnership with team protegée Lewis Hamilton at McLaren, and Räikkönen filled Schumacher's big boots at Ferrari.

Räikkönen and Alonso started the season well and were dominant until Hamilton took his first victory in a stop-start crash-hit race in Canada. Hamilton won again in the United States before Räikkönen's season came back to life with wins in France and Britain. Räikkönen came back from 17 points behind and went on to win in Brazil and take the title by a point as Hamilton struggled to seventh.

2008

McLaren and Ferrari renewed their rivalry as Hamilton and Massa raced to another nail-bitingly tight title decider. Meanwhile, Alonso returned to Renault in a season that welcomed a new street circuit in Valencia and a night race in Singapore.

Kovalainen won in Hungary, but Massa dominated in Valencia and won again in the Belgian rain after Hamilton was disqualified for an illegal move in a battle with Räikkönen.

Italy saw a shock victory for Toro Rosso and Sebastian Vettel then Alonso won the night race in Singapore and the Japan Grand Prix where Massa and Hamilton collided. Massa won a thrilling race in Brazil and thought he had the title when Hamilton was sixth on the last lap, but the Briton made a last-gasp pass and stole the title by a point.

>>>>

Right: Jenson Button celebrates on the podium after winning the 2009 Spanish Grand Prix.

2009

The introduction of Kinetic Energy recovery System (KERS) and return of slick tyres made for an exciting season.

The season now stretched to 17 races starting in Australia and ending at the brand new circuit in Abu Dhabi. Ferrari and McLaren struggled to find form, and new constructor Brawn swept in. Button dominated the season, finally securing the title at the Brazilian Grand Prix. Brawn became the first constructor to win the constructors Championship in a debut season. Button became the 10th British driver to win the Championship.

2010

The 2010 season saw the introduction of a new track in Korea and drivers competing in 19 races overall.

Red Bull made an impressive comeback after failing to make their mark in the previous season. Red Bull went on to win the championship with their driver, Vettel, securing the driver's title after a tough battle with Button during the final race of the season at Abu Dhabi. Vettel became the youngest driver ever to win the championship. The 2010 season also saw world champion, Schumacher, come out of retirement.

2011

Vettell successfully defended his title in style winning the opening race after qualifying in pole position. He went on to emphatic wins in Malaysia, China, Turkey and Spain, but Button was close behind.

The championship came to a head in Japan where Vettel qualified just nine-thousandths of a second faster than Button for pole. Button went on to win the race, but Vettel made a podium finish, which was enough to secure the title for another year. During the last race of the season Vettel broke Mansell's record by securing his 15th pole position of the season.

Above: Hamilton takes the checkered flag to claim his maiden victory at the 2007 Canadian Grand Prix.

2012

2012 saw Vettell winning his third title for Red Bull by three points in the incident-packed Brazilian Grand Prix, making Vettell the youngest driver ever to win three world titles.

The huge 20-race season started as usual in Australia with a return to form from Alonso, but he was beaten by Button, who took an early lead from his team-mate, Hamilton. Alonso came back in Malaysia to steal the victory from Perez and Hamilton, who qualified in pole position once again. Vettel finished outside of the points and the championship looked wide open. Mercedes' controversial DRS design saw Nico Rosberg take pole and the victory for Mercedes and their first win as a constructor since 1955 in China. Despite political unrest and calls from human rights campaigners, including Amnesty International, for the race to be boycotted, the Bahrain Grand Prix went ahead and heralded a return to form from Vettel, who took the win and secured a lead at the top of the championship. Vettel capitalized on this victory by going on to win the championship.

Below: Jenson Button (Brawn BGP001 Mercedes) on his way to victory in the 2009 Spanish Grand Prix.

F1

Index

 F1

Picture credits

The publisher would like to thank the following for permission to reproduce the following copyright material:

GETTY IMAGES

• AFP/Getty Images 6-7, 98-99, 104-105, 116, 118-119, 122-123, 126, 130-131, 134, 142-143, 144, 145, 150-151, 156, 166-167,

169, 171, 173

• Bongarts/Getty Images 102-103

• Getty Images 158

LAT PHOTOGRAPHIC

• Colin McMaster/LAT Photographic 8-9, 14

• Lorenzo Bellanca/LAT Photographic 15, 16-17, 75, 172

• Charles Coates/LAT Photographic 18, 19, 52-53, 59, 62-63, 78, 79, 80, 95, 98-99, 154, 155, 157, 159, 161

• Steve Etherington/LAT Photographic 22, 23, 74, 76-77, 81, 160, 162-163, 168-169

• Tim Clarke/LAT Photographic 26-27, 30-31, 34-35

• Andrew Ferraro/LAT Photographic 38-39, 84-85

• Glenn Dunbar/LAT Photographic 42-43, 44-45, 48, 70-71, 90, 91, 92

• Jeff Bloxham/LAT Photographic 44

• Tony Smythe/ LAT Photographic 49, 108-109, 110-111, 112-113, 114-115, 117

• Steven Tee/LAT Photographic 80, 82-83, 106-107, 120, 124-125, 128-129, 132-133, 135, 137, 138-139, 140-141, 145, 149, 152-153

• Andrew Ferraro/LAT Photographic 86-87

• Michael Cooper/LAT Photographic 164-165

• Philip Lange 10

• Sophie James 11

• Dr Ajay Kumar Singh 20

• Elzbin 28

• Jean Vaillancourt 36

• Natursports 88

• Morozova Tatiana 72

SHUTTERSTOCK.COM (Sh)

Background images throughout the book: Sh/ © wongwean, Sh/ © Harley Molesworth, Sh/ © Jiripravda,

Sh/ © Factor41, Sh/ © Ola-ola, Sh/ © Sergej Khakimullin.

1c Sh/ © Julie Lucht.